E S T A T E   P U B L I C A T I O N S

WATFORD · HEMEL

RICKMANSWORTH · BUSHEY · NORTH
KINGS LANGLEY · CH(

C000083598

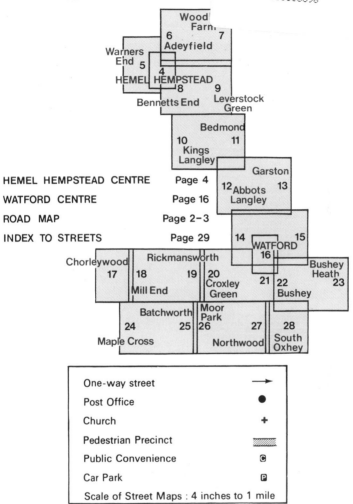

HEMEL HEMPSTEAD CENTRE	Page 4
WATFORD CENTRE	Page 16
ROAD MAP	Page 2-3
INDEX TO STREETS	Page 29

One-way street →
Post Office ●
Church +
Pedestrian Precinct ▨
Public Convenience ⒞
Car Park ⒫

Scale of Street Maps : 4 inches to 1 mile

Street plans prepared and published by ESTATE PUBLICATIONS, Bridewell House, Tenterden, Kent and based upon the ORDNANCE SURVEY maps with the sanction of the controller of H.M. Stationery Office.

The publishers acknowledge the co-operation of Hertsmere Borough Council, Watford District Council, Three Rivers District Council and Dacorum District Council in the preparation of these maps.

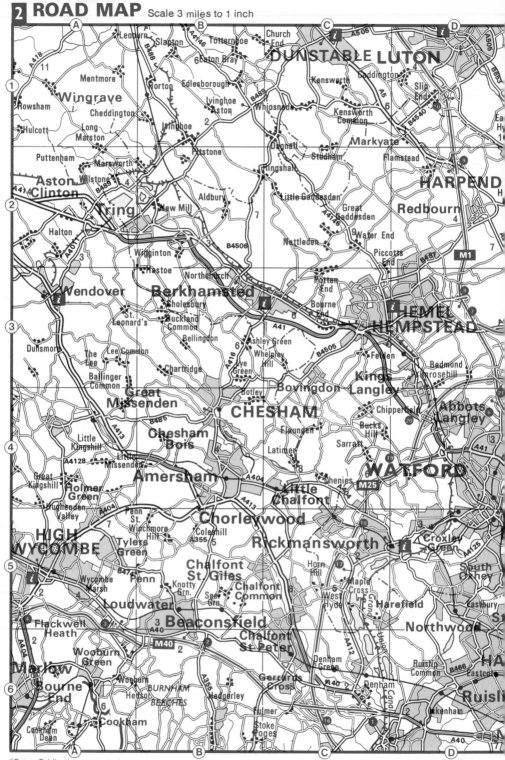

2 ROAD MAP   Scale 3 miles to 1 inch

©Estate Publications

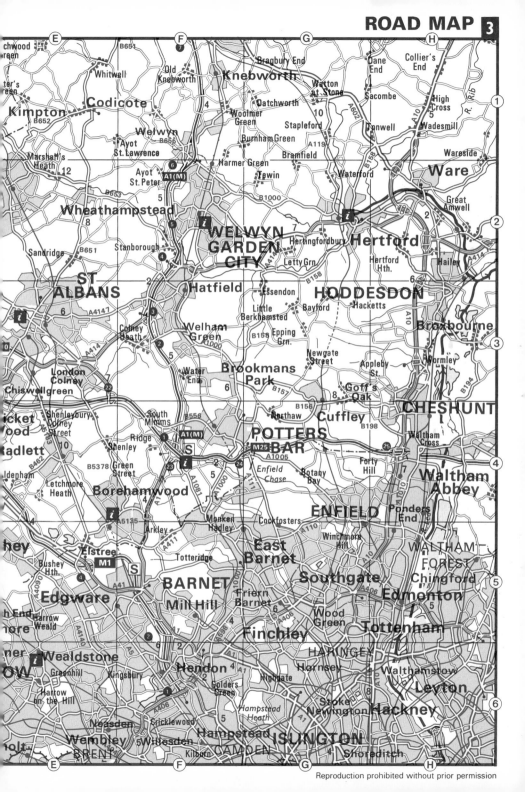

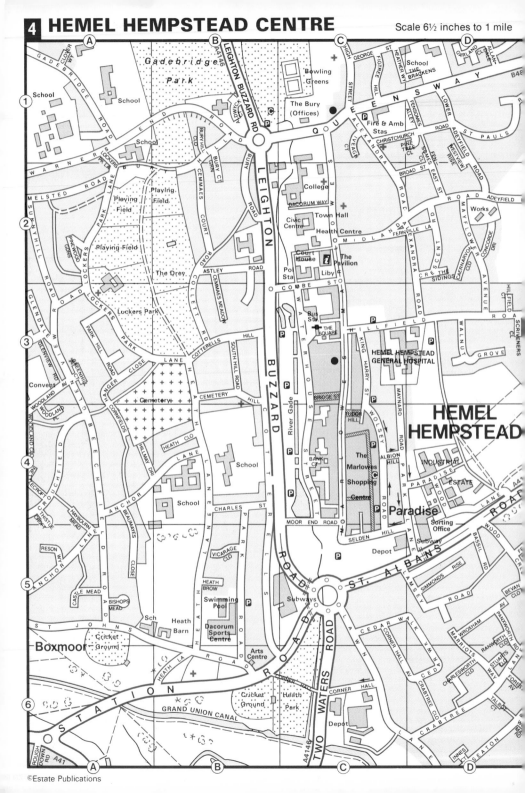

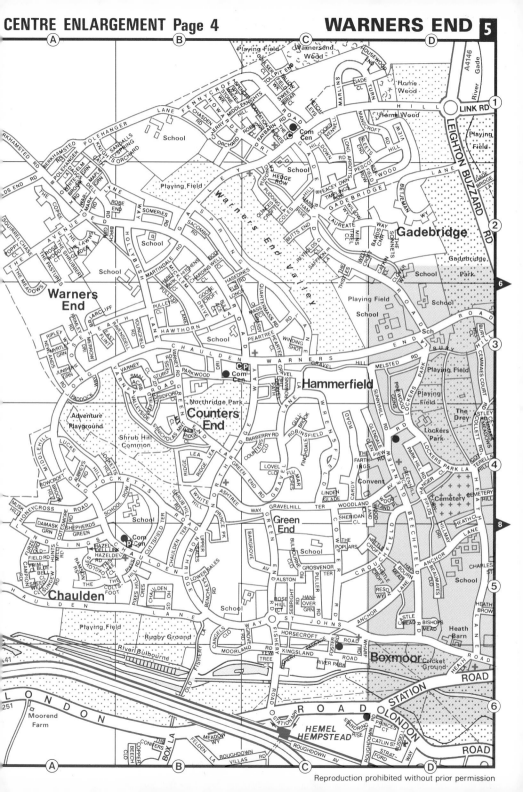

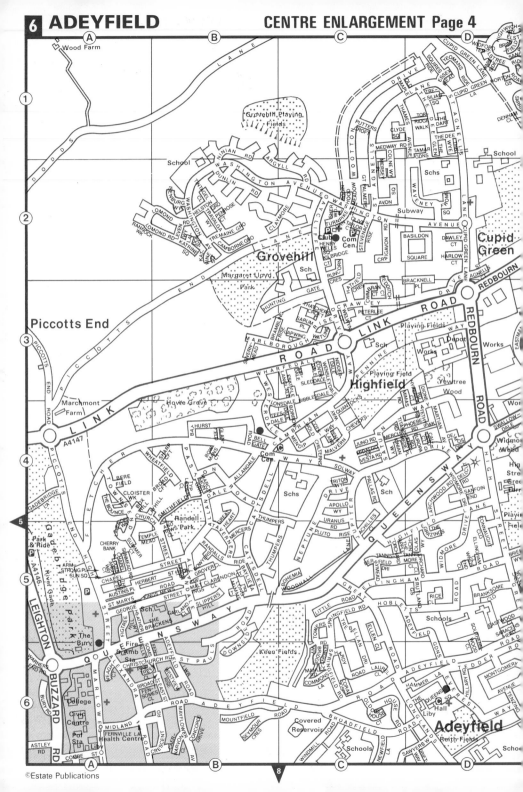

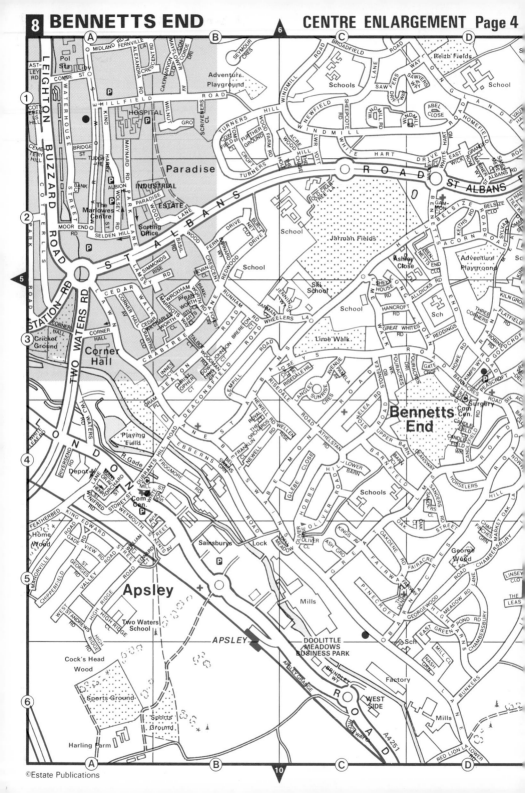

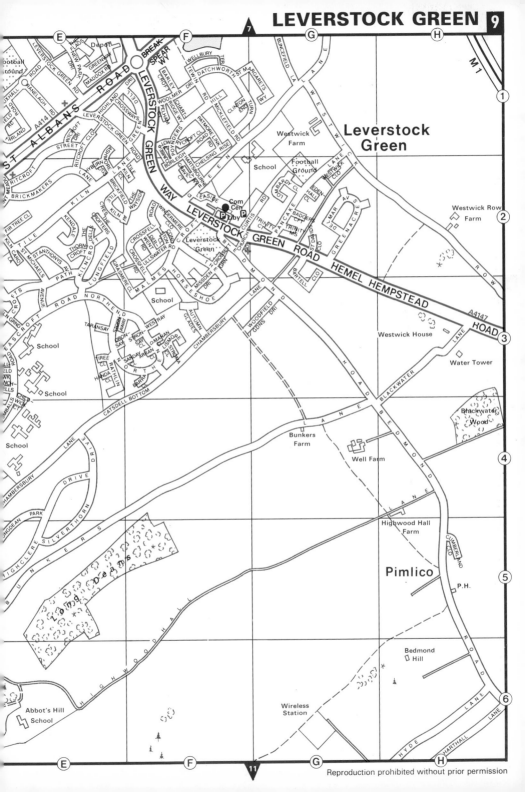

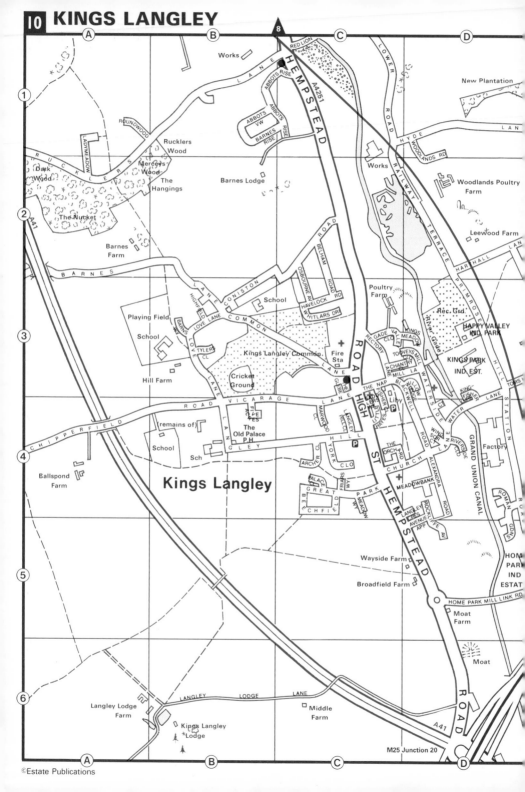

Kings Langley

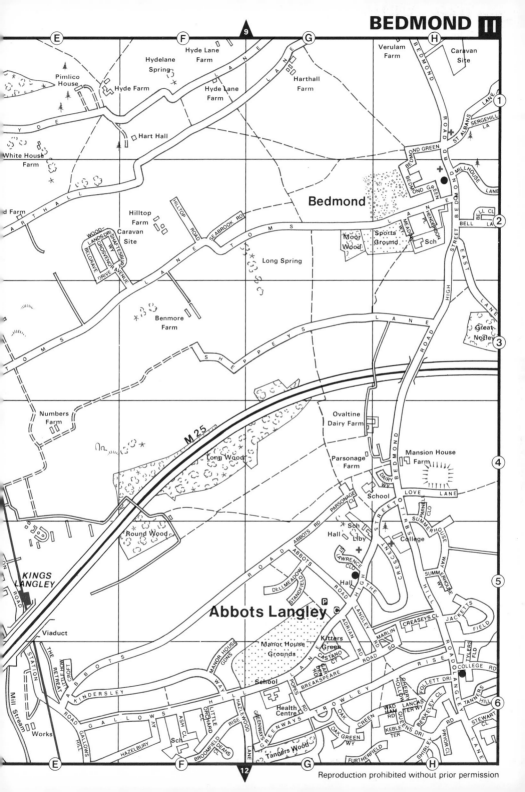

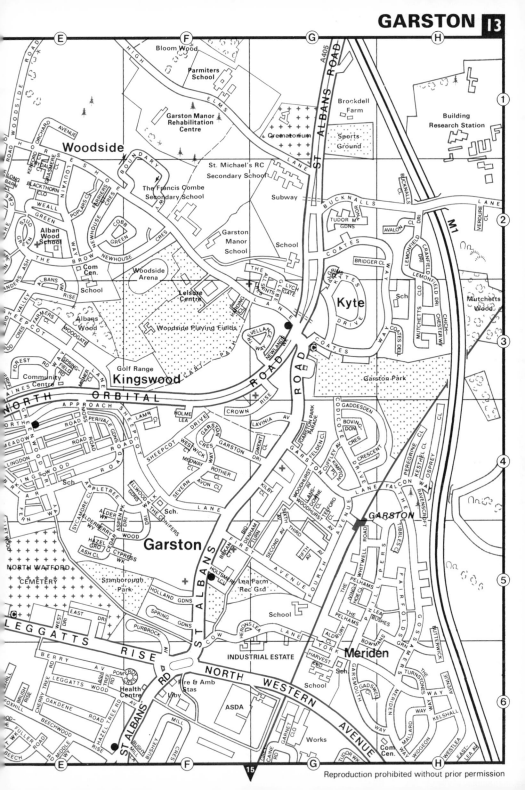

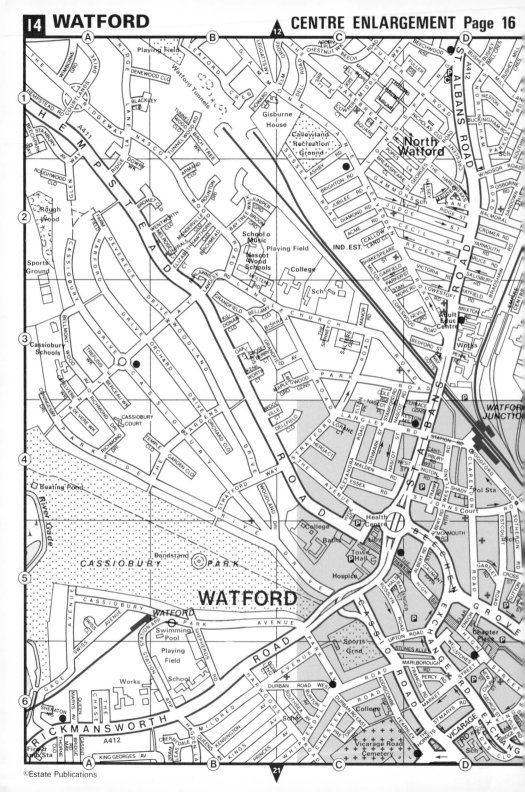

© Estate Publications

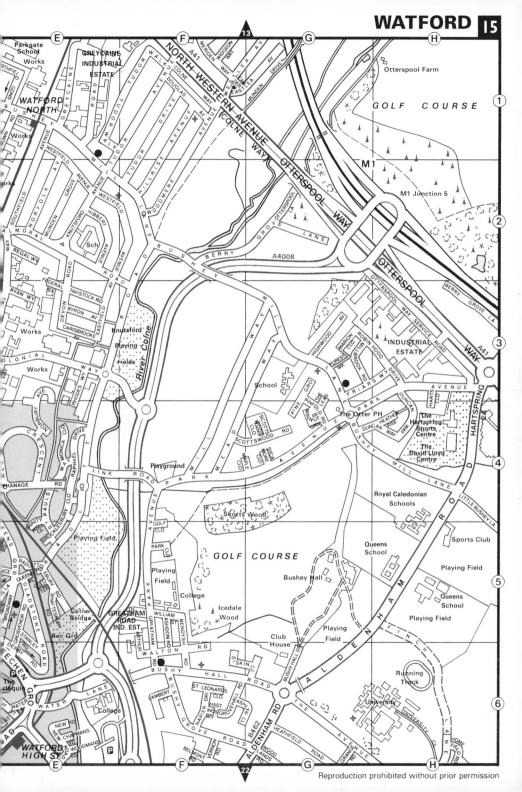

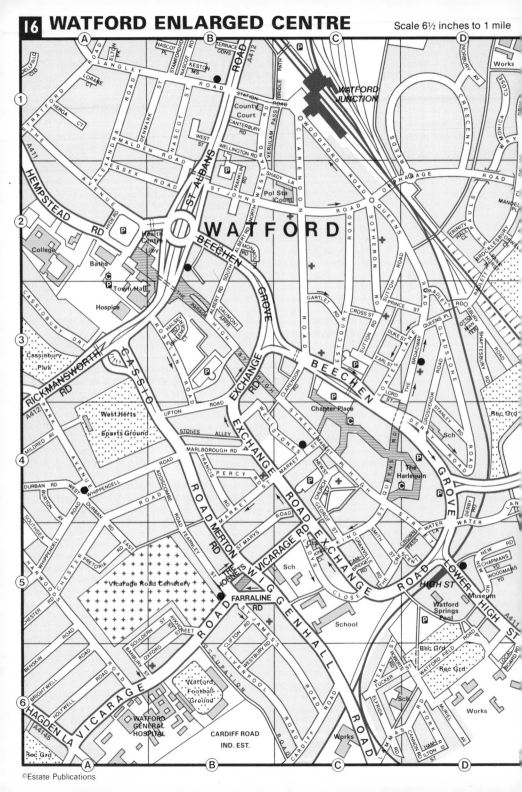

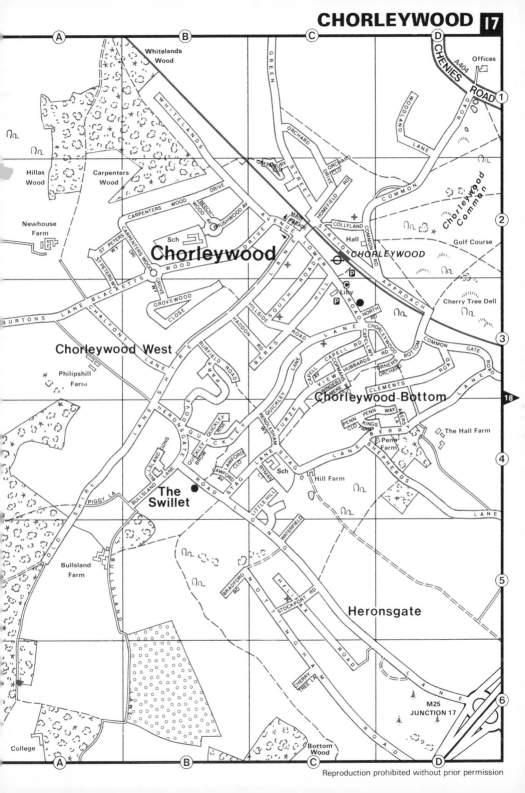

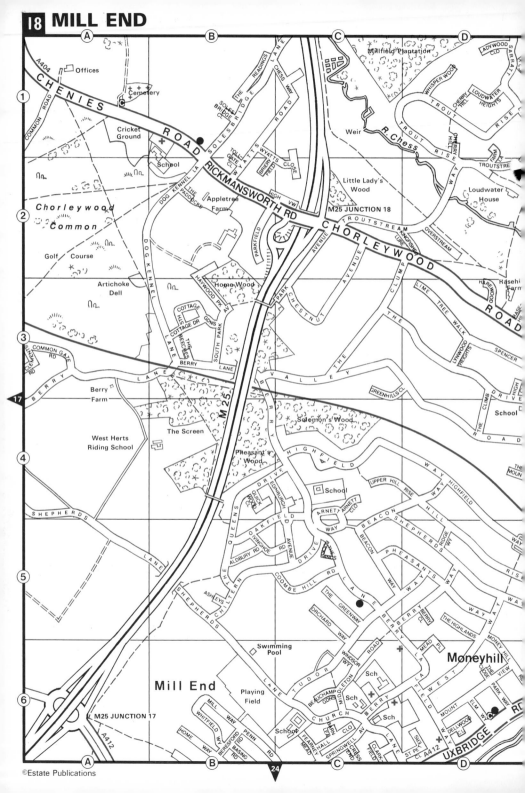

Upper Plantation

BRIDLE LANE
LOWER PLANTATION

Round Spring Farm

Loudwater

WAGON WY

LOUDWATER RIDGE

TIMBER RIDGE

ARMITAGE CLO

LODGE DRIVE

ROOKS HILL

CHESS HILL

LOUDWATER CHESS LANE

LOUDWATER LANE

LOUDWATER DRIVE

Loudwater Farm

R. Chess

Redheath Nursery

Thurlwood House

Parrot's Dell

Croxley Green

Copthorne Wood

Little Gillions

SARRATT ROAD

ROAD LITTLE GREEN LANE

LITTLE GREEN LANE

Croxley House

Killingdown Farm

THE GREEN LANE

THE GREEN

LITTLE GREEN

DUG LOVATTS

BALDWINS

WHITE GATES CL

GROVE CRES

Recreation Ground

OWENS WAY

CHENIES WAY

PHIHWICK WALK

COPTHORNE CLO

ROAD

OLD BARN LA

School

Sports Ground

Playing Field

WALK

THE DRIVE

ALLEY

CHORLEYWOOD RD

Rickmansworth Masonic School

Nurseries

Watercress Beds

MILLTHORNE GREEN LA

CLO

ELMCOTE WAY

CHESSVALE RD

UPLANDS

WINDMILL DRIVE

COPTHORNE DRIVE

THE HERONS

NEW ROAD

YORKE RD

DICKINSON AV

A412

Sch

WATFORD RD

BATEMAN RD

Sch

Playing Fields

Mill

Sports Ground

Football Ground

RICKMANSWORTH

ROAD SCOTS

CHAMBERS COTTAGE

LAVROCK LA

ALL SAINTS

Sch

Sch

Playing Fields

Croxleyhall Wood

THE MOUNT

HIGH FIELD WAY

WINCHFIELD WAY

DRIVE

NIGHTINGALE RD

CHORLEYWOOD RD

VICTORIA RD

Camp

Playing Field

Rickmansworth Park

Sch

PARK

STREET

RICKMANSWORTH BY-PASS

CARAVAN LA

Works

Croxleyhall Farm

THRUSH GRN

SWAL LOW WAY

NIGHTINGALE RD

TOWNFIELD

CEDARS AV

NIGHTINGALE RD

RICKMANSWORTH

Fire & Amb Stas

Pol Sta

RECTORY RD

PARSONAGE RD

HOMESTEAD

RECTORY LA

STATION RD

NORTHW

PC

Liby

HIGH

Watersmeet Centre

THE CLOISTERS

WHARF LA

Sch

Fortune Common

RIVERSIDE

UXBRIDGE RD

R. Colne

HIGH STREET

WENSUM

EBURY RD

DORAL MEADO

BURY MEADOWS

BURY LA

CHURCH STREET

TALBOT

NORFOLK RD

SKIDMORE WAY

WATERSON RD

Works

A404 DRIVE

Batchworth Lake

Grand Union Canal

Hampton Hall Farm

MOOR LA

E F G H
1 2 3 20 4 5 6
25

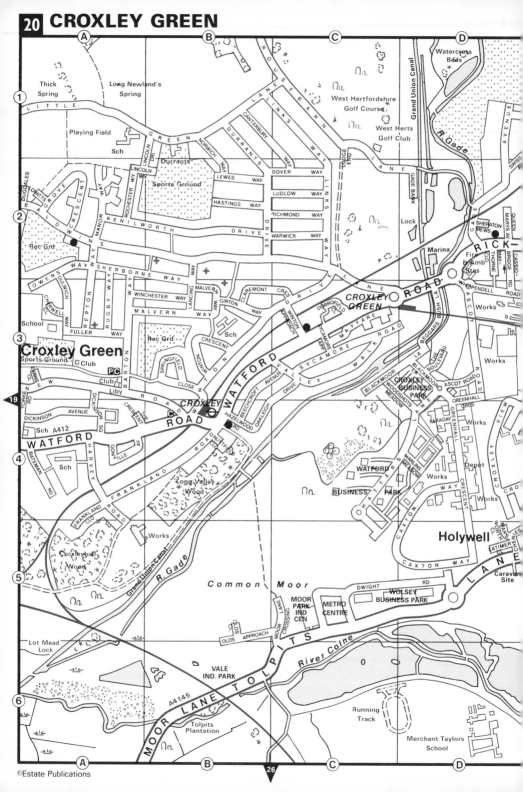

Thick Spring

Long Newland's Spring

Playing Field

Sch

LITTLE

GREEN CROFT

LINCOLN

DUGGDALES

COATS GROVE

BALDWIN CRESCENT

MANOR WAY

KENILWORTH DRIVE

ROCHESTER WY

LINCOLN WY

NORWICH WAY

CANTERBURY

DURRANTS

Durrants

Sports Ground

LEWES WAY

HASTINGS WAY

LANE

LINKS WAY

ROUSEBARN

LINKS LANE

LANE

DOVER WAY

LUDLOW WAY

RICHMOND WAY

WARWICK WAY

DRIVE

West Hertfordshire Golf Course

West Herts Golf Club

Grand Union Canal

R. Gade

GADE BANK

LANE

QUEEN

MARYS AV

SWISS

AVENUE

Lock

Marina

RICK-

SHERATON MEWS

Fire & Amb Stas

THORNE

BRIDGE WAY

CASSIO-

OPPENDELL

Works

SCOT

ROAD

OWENS WAY

DULWICH WAY

CHERWELL WAY

REPTON WAY

RUGBY WAY

SHERBORNE WAY

WINCHESTER WAY

MALVERN WAY

FULLER WAY

School

Rec Grd

LANCING WAY

MALVERN

GIRTON WAY

Sch

CRESCENT

WINTON

CLAREMONT CRES

APPROACH

DORROFIELD

SYCAMORE APP

MAYFARE

CROXLEY GREEN

ROAD

WALK ROAD

BEGGARS BUSH LA

BLACKMOOR

CROXLEY BUSINESS PARK

WOODSHOTS

MEADOW

THE BOULEVARD

ASCOT ROAD

GREENHALL CRES

FARADAY

GREENHALL

Works

Works

CROXLEY VIEW

CROX

Croxley Green

Sports Ground

Club

PC

Club

Liby

EVANS

ORKE

RD

DICKINSON AVENUE

Sch A412

BATEMAN RD

HARVEY

Sch

BARTON WAY

SPRINGFIELD

CRESCENT

THE CRESCENT

DICKINSON SQ

GONVILLE AV

CLOSE

WINTON

CROXLEY

WATFORD

ROAD

CROXLEY

HAZELWOOD

NUTFIELD RD

BEECHCROFT

AVENUE

OAKLEIGH

WATFORD

SYCAMORE DRIVE

ILEY

DRIVE

WATFORD BUSINESS PARK

HASTE

MARLINS MEADOW

CAXTON WAY

Works

Works

Depot

Works

MARLINS

LATIMER

CHENIES

WATFORD

Sch

FRANKLAND CLO

FRANKLAND ROAD

Works

Long Valley Wood

Croxleyhall Wood

Grand Union Canal

R. Gade

Holywell

CAXTON WAY

Caravan Site

Common Moor

DWIGHT RD

WOLSEY BUSINESS PARK

MOOR PARK IND CEN

METRO CENTRE

LANE

CROSSING

MOOR LANE

LANE

Lot Mead Lock

OLDS

OLDS APPROACH

TOLPITS

River Colne

Running Track

Merchant Taylors School

MOOR LANE

A4145

VALE IND. PARK

Tolpits Plantation

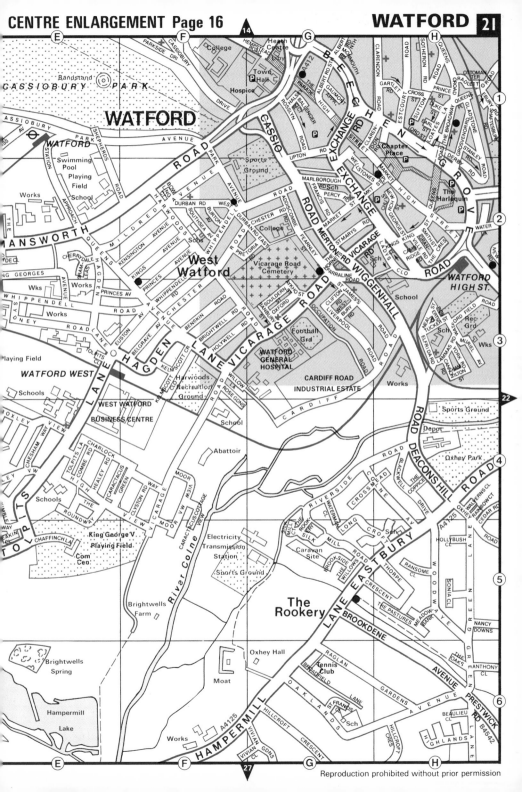

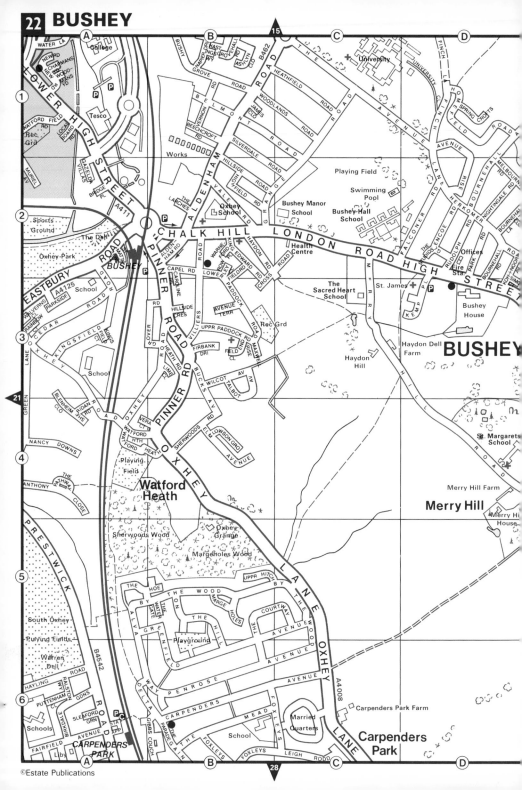

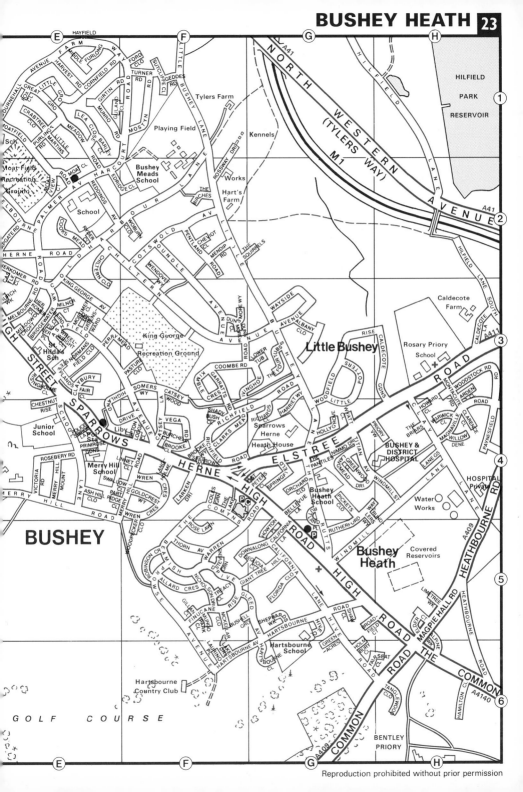

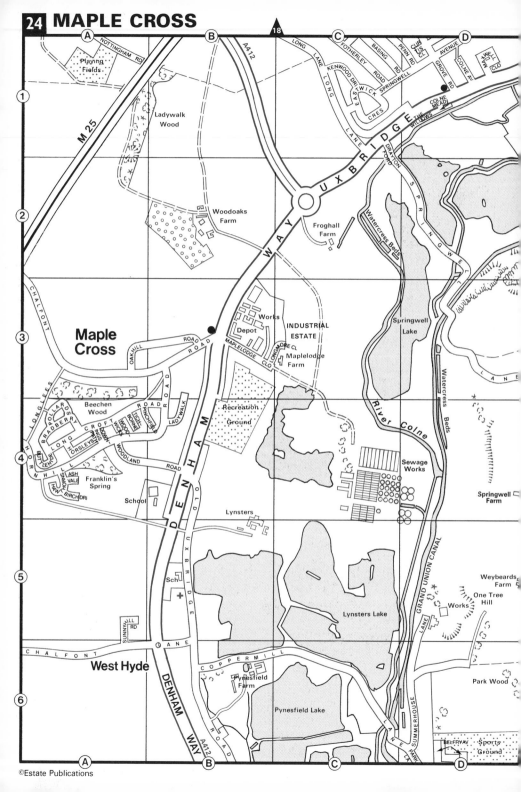

24 MAPLE CROSS

Maple Cross

West Hyde

©Estate Publications

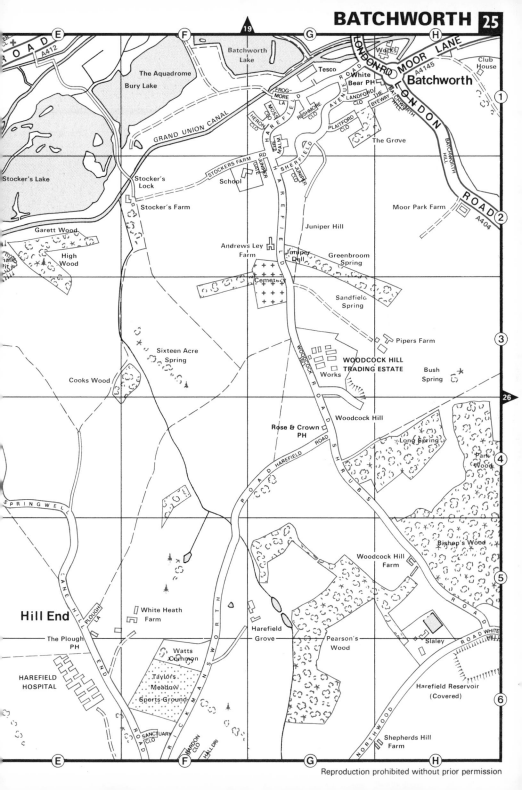

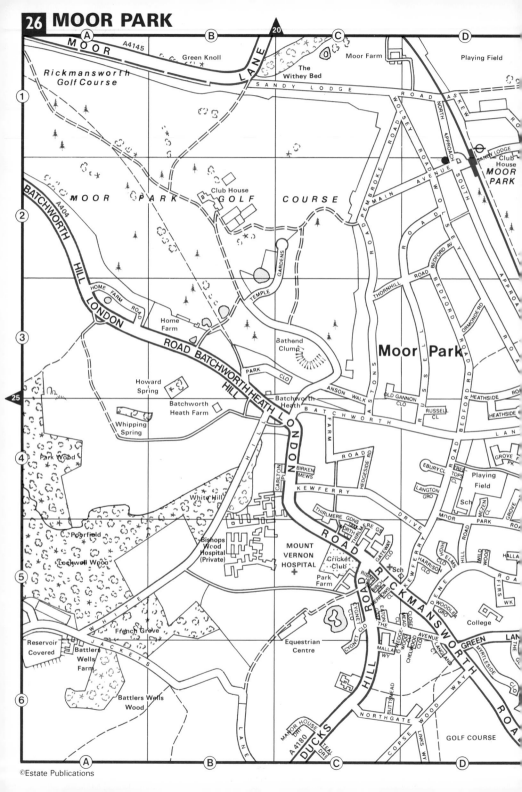

21

E F G H

HILLCROFT CRES

HAMPERMILL LA

Manor of the Rose

South Oxhey Playing Fields

Ox Pasture Spring

①

Hampermill Wood

South Oxhey Playing Fields

Big Wood

SIDMOUTH CLO
FULFORD
GROVE
NEW
HAREWOOD

Round Spring

HAMILTON
DRIVE

Hampermill Spring

ASHBURNHAM
HALLOWES CRES

ARBROATH

HOLMSIDE RD

ANDY LODGE GOLF COURSE

CULVERDEN

Sch ②

The Rough

Old Furze Field

Young Hangings

Little Furze Field

Schs

South Oxhey

Eastbury

School

OXHEY WOODS

Old Hangings

Beck Mason's Wood

MUIRFIELD GREEN
MAYLANDS

③

The Plantation

O X H E Y WOODS

Offices

NORTHWOOD HEADQUARTERS

OXHEY RISE CL

THE WOODS

PRESTWICK

28

ROAD

④

Bracken Hill House

Oxhey Woods

Wild Woods

MARKAB RD

Pocklington House

SEVEN ACRES

Admiralty House

Reservoir (covered)

⑤

RAVENSWOOD

Pinner Hill Golf Club

School

Northwood

Liby

PARK VIEW ROAD

WATFORD LANE

WOODGATE CRES

SHERTON RISE

NORTHWOOD

Pol Sta

HIGH ST CHURCH RD

Northwood

TOWNSEND WAY

CHURCH RD

HILLSIDE

WAY

POTTERHEIGHTS CLO

⑥

A4125

EMMANUEL RD

HILLSIDE RISE

HILLSIDE GDNS

PINNER HILL ROAD

E F G H

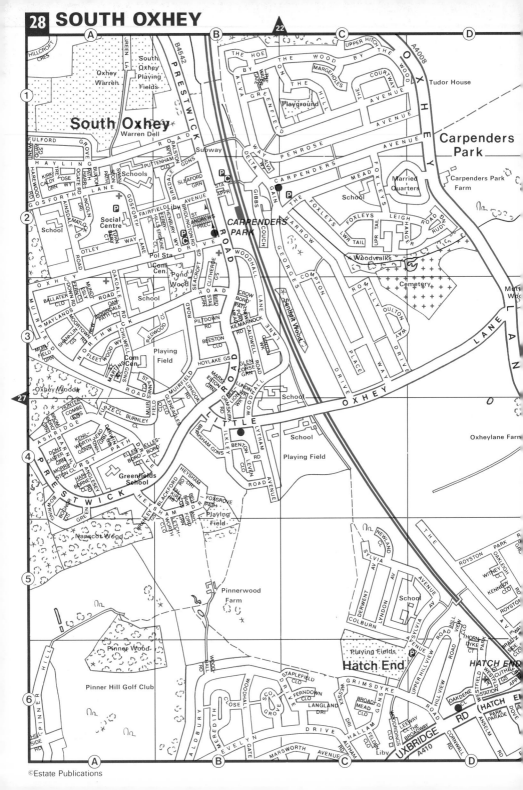

HEMEL HEMPSTEAD

Street	Ref
Abbots Rise	10 B1
Abbots Vw	10 B1
Abel Clo	8 D1
Achilles Clo	6 C5
Acorn Rd	8 D2
Acre Wood	8 C1
Adeyfield Gdns	6 D5
Adeyfield Rd	6 B6
Airdale	6 C3
Albion Hill	4 C4
Aldwyck Ct	4 B1
Alexandra Rd, Hemel Hempstead	4 C1
Alexandra Rd, Kings Langley	10 D4
Allandale	6 B4
Alldicks Rd	8 D3
Alston Rd	5 C5
Anchor La	4 A5
Andrews Clo	6 B5
Apollo Way	6 C4
Apsley Grange	8 C6
Aragon Clo	7 F1
Archer Rd	10 C4
Archway Ct	6 A5
Argyll Rd	6 C2
Arkley Rd	7 E1
Armstrong Pl	6 A5
Arran Clo	9 F3
Arundel Clo	7 E6
Ash Gro	8 C5
Ashby Ct	7 E1
Ashmore Gdns	9 E2
Ashtree Way	5 B4
Aspfield Row	5 D2
Astley Rd	4 B2
Aston View	6 D1
Athelstan Rd	8 C4
Aubreys Rd	5 A4
Austins Pl	6 A5
Autumn Glades	9 F3
Avenue App	10 D5
Avia Clo	8 B4
Avon Sq	6 C2
Aycliffe Dri	6 C2
Badgers Croft	9 C2
Bank Ct	4 C4
Barberry Rd	5 C4
Bards Corner	5 D2
Bargrove Av	5 C5
Barley Croft	9 F1
Barn Clo	8 C4
Barnacres Rd	8 D3
Barnard Way	8 B2
Barnes La	10 A2
Barnes Rise	10 B1
Barns Way	10 B3
Barnfield	8 C4
Barra Clo	9 F3
Bartell Clo	9 G2
Basil Rd	4 D5
Basildon Sq	6 D2
Bathurst Rd	6 B4
Bayford Clo	7 F1
Baylie Ct	6 B5
Baylie La	6 B5
Beaumayes Clo	4 A4
Bedmond Rd	9 F2
Beechfield	10 C4
Beechfield Rd	4 A4
Belham Rd	10 C2
Bell Gate	6 B4
Belmont Rd	8 B4
Belsize Clo	8 D2
Belsize Rd	8 D2
Belswains Grn	8 B4
Belswains Lya	8 B4
Benchleys Rd	5 B5
Bennetts End Clo	8 D2
Bennetts End Rd	8 D2
Berefield	6 A4
Berkeley Sq	7 F1
Berkhamsted Rd	5 A1
Berrymead	6 C5
Betjeman Way	5 D2
Bevan Clo	4 D5
Birch Grn	5 A2
Birch Leys	7 F1
Bishops Mead	4 A5
Blackwater La	9 H3
Blackwell Rd	10 C3
Blair Clo	7 E1
Bluebell Clo	5 A5
Bodwell Clo	5 B2
Bohemia	6 C5
Boleyn Clo	7 F1
Borrowdale	6 C4
Botley Rd	7 E1
Boundary Way	7 F3
Bowmans Ct	6 B4
Bowyers	6 B5
Box La	5 B6
Boxhill	6 A4
Boxted Rd	5 A2
Bracknell Pl	6 D3
Braemar Turn	7 E1
Brambling Rise	6 B3
Bramfield Pl	6 D1
Bransome Clo	6 D5
Breakspear Way	7 F6
Brereton Ct	8 B3
Briarcliff	5 A3
Brickfield Av	9 E2
Brickmakers La	9 E2
Bridge St	4 C3
Briery Ct	7 E5
Briery Way	6 D5
Brindley Way	8 C6
Broad Croft	6 B4
Broad St	4 D2
Broadfield Rd	6 C6
Bronte Cres	7 E1
Broom Hill	5 A4
Bulbourne Clo	5 C5
Bullace Clo	5 B3
Buncefield La	7 F3
Bunkers La	8 D6
Burleigh Rd	9 F2
Burnet Clo	8 B2
Burns Dri	7 E1
Bury Ct	4 B2
Bury Grn	4 B1
Bury Hill	4 A2
Bury Hill Clo	4 B1
Bury Rd	4 B1
Butts End	5 C2
Byron Pl	7 E1
Caernarvon Clo	4 D2
Callisto Ct	6 D4
Camborne Gro	6 D4
Cambrian Way	6 C4
Campion Rd	5 A5
Candlefield Clo	8 D4
Candlefield Rd	8 D4
Candlefield Walk	8 D4
Cangels Clo	5 B5
Cardy Rd	5 C4
Caro La	9 E2
Castle Mead	4 A5
Catherine Clo	7 F1
Catkin Clo	5 D2
Catlin St	5 D6
Catsdell Bottom	9 E4
Cattsdell	6 B5
Cedar Walk	4 C5
Cemetery Hill	4 B3
Cemmaes Court Rd	4 B2
Cemmaes Meadow	4 B2
Chaffinches Grn	8 D5
Chalfont Clo	7 E2
Chambersbury La	8 D5
Chantry La	10 C3
Chapel Cotts	6 A5
Chapel St	6 A5
Chardins Clo	5 B2
Charles St	4 B4
Charlesworth Clo	4 D6
Chartridge Way	9 F1
Chasden Rd	5 B1
Chaucer Walk	7 E1
Chaulden Ho Gdns	5 B5
Chaulden La	5 A5
Chaulden Ter	5 B5
Chelsing Rise	9 F2
Chenies Ct	7 E1
Cherry Bank	6 A5
Cherry Orchard	5 B1
Cherrytree La	7 F1
Cheviots	6 C4
Childwick Ct	9 E3
Chilterns	6 C4
Chipperfield Rd, Apsley	8 A5
Chipperfield Rd, Kings Langley	10 A4
Christchurch Rd	4 C1
Christopher St	8 B3
Church La	10 C4
Church Rd	9 F2
Church St	4 A4
Clarendon Clo	6 B5
Claymore	6 C2
Cleveland Rd	7 E4
Cleveland Way	7 E4
Cleves Rd	7 E1
Clinton End	9 F1
Cloister Walk	6 A4
Clover Way	4 A1
Clyde Sq	6 C1
Codicote Row	7 E1
Coleridge Cres	7 E1
Coles Hill	5 C2
Collett Rd	4 B2
Colne Way	6 C1
Combe St	4 C3
Common La	10 B3
Commons La	6 C6
Concorde Dri	4 D2
Coniston Clo	9 F2
Coniston Rd	10 B3
Connaught Gro	6 D5
Cooks Vennell	5 C1
Copper Beech Clo	5 B6
Coral Gdns	6 C6
Corner Hall	4 C6
Corner Hall Av	4 C5
Cornfields	4 A4
Cotswold	6 C4
Cotterells	4 B4
Cotterells Hill	4 B3
Cottesmore Rd	5 A5
Coulser Clo	5 C1
Counters Clo	5 C4
Coverdale	6 C3
Cowper Rd	5 C5
Coxfield Clo	8 B1
Crabtree Clo	4 D6
Crabtree La	4 D6
Crackley Meadow	7 E2
Craigavon Rd	6 C2
Crawley Dri	6 C3
Crescent Rd	4 D2
Crest Pk	7 F5
Crofts Path	9 E3
Crossett Grn	9 F2
Crossfell Rd	9 F2
Crossways	9 E1
Crouchfield	4 A4
Cuffley Ct	7 F1
Cumberland Clo	9 H5
Cumberlow Pl	9 F1
Cupid Green La	6 D2
Curtis Rd	9 F2
Cuttsfield Ter	5 B5
Cwmbran Ct	6 C3
Dacorum Way	4 C2
Daggs Dell Rd	5 A2
Damask Grn	5 A5
Darwin Clo	7 E1
Datchet Clo	7 E1
Datchworth Turn	9 F1
Dawley Ct	6 D2
Deaconsfield Rd	8 B4
Deansway	8 D4
Deimos Dri	6 D4
Dell Meadow	8 C5
Dellcut Rd	6 D4
Delmar Av	9 G2
Denham Clo	6 D1
Derwent Rd	9 F2
Dickens Ct	7 E1
Dione Rd	6 D3
Dodds La	6 A2
Dowling Ct	8 B3
Downside	6 B6
Driftway	8 C1
Dunlin Rd	6 B2
Dunster Rd	7 E1
Durrants Hill Rd	8 A4
Duxons Turn	7 E5
East Green	8 D5
East Mimms	6 B5
East St	4 D2
Eastflint	5 A3
Eastman Way	6 D3
Eastwick Row	8 D1
Eastwood Ct	6 D5
Eaton Rd	7 E4
Ebberns Rd	8 B4
Edenhall Clo	9 G2
Edward Ct	8 A5
Ellen Clo	6 C5
Ellingham Clo	6 D5
Ellingham Rd	6 C5
Elm Grn	5 A2
Elstree Rd	6 D1
Epping Grn	7 E1
Eskdale	6 C3
Essex Mead	6 D1
Europa Rd	6 D4
Everest Way	6 D6
Fairacre	8 D5
Fairway	8 C5
Fairway Ct	8 D5
Fallowfield Walk	5 C1
Farland Rd	9 E1
Feacey Down	5 C2
Featherbed La	8 A5
Felden La	5 B6
Fennycroft Rd	5 B1
Fensomes Alley	4 D1
Fensomes Clo	4 D1
Fern Dri	4 D5
Fernville La	4 D2
Field Rd	9 E1
Fields End Rd	5 A2
Figtree Hill	4 C1
Finchdale	5 C4
Finway Rd	7 E2
Fir Tree Clo	9 E2
Fisher Clo	10 C3
Fishery Pass	5 C6
Fishery Rd	5 C5
Five Acres	10 B4
Flatfield Rd	8 D3
Fletcher Way	6 A5
Forest Av	4 D6
Foster Rd	5 C6
Fouracres Dri	8 D3
Fouracres Walk	8 C3
Franklin Clo	8 B4
Friars Way	10 C4
Frimley Rd	5 A3
Frogmore Rd	8 B4
Frome Sq	6 D2
Fulmar Cres	5 C4
Furlongs	5 B3
Further Ground	8 B1
Furze Rd	5 A5
Gade Clo	5 C1
Gade Valley Clo	10 C3
Gade View Rd	8 A5
Gadebridge La	5 C2
Gadebridge Rd	4 A1
Galley Hill	5 B2
Gammon Clo	8 D2
Gannymede Pl	6 D3
Garland Clo	4 D1
Gate Croft	8 D3
George St	4 C1
Georgewood Rd	8 D5
Glamis Clo	7 E1
Glanfield	6 B4
Glebe Clo	8 C4
Glen View Rd	4 A3
Glendale	4 A3
Goldcroft	8 D3
Goose Croft	5 B3
Grange Clo	8 D1
Grasmere Clo	9 E2
Grassy Clo	5 C3
Gravel Hill	5 C3
Gravel La	5 C4
Gravel Path	5 C3
Gravelhill Ter	5 C4
Gravely Ct	9 F2
Great Elms Rd	8 C5

Great Heart 6 B5
Great Palmers 6 C2
Great Park 10 C4
Great Rd 6 C5
Great Sturgess Rd 5 B3
Great Whites Rd 8 C3
Green Dell 9 F1
Green End La 5 B3
Green End Rd 5 B4
Green La 9 F2
Greenacres 9 G2
Greenhill Ct 4 A3
Greenway 7 E6
Grosvenor Ter 5 C5
Grove Rd 5 C5
Grover Clo 6 B5
Gullbrook 5 C4

Haddon Clo 8 D2
Hales Pk 7 F5
Hales Park Clo 7 F5
Haleswood Rd 7 E6
Half Moon Meadow 7 F2
Hall Rd 7 E4
Hammer La 6 D6
Hancroft Rd 8 C3
Handa Clo 9 E3
Hanger Clo 4 A3
Hanover Grn 5 C5
Hardy Rd 6 C6
Hare Park Clo 5 B2
Harlow Ct 6 D2
Harthall La 10 D2
Hartsbourne Way 9 F2
Hasedines Rd 5 B2
Hatfield Cres 6 C3
Havelock Rd 10 C3
Hawthorn La 5 B3
Haybourne Mead 4 A4
Hazeldell Link 5 A5
Hazeldell Rd 5 A5
Heath Brow 4 B5
Heath Clo 4 B4
Heath La 4 B3
Heather Way 4 C1
Hedge Row 5 C2
Helston Gro 6 B2
Hemel Hempstead Rd 9 G2
Hempstead Rd 10 C1
Henry St 8 A4
Henry Wells Sq 6 C2
Herbert St 6 A5
Hetchleys 5 C1
High Ridge Clo 8 A5
High Ridge Rd 8 A5
High St, Hemel Hempstead 4 C1
High St, Kings Langley 10 C4
High Street Grn 6 D4
High Wych Way 6 D1
Highbarns 8 D5
Highclere Dri 9 E5
Highfield 10 B3
Highfield La 6 C5
Highland Dri 9 E1
Highwood Hall La 9 E6
Hill Common 8 D4
Hillary Rd 6 D6
Hilldown Rd 5 C1
Hillfield Ct 4 D3
Hillfield Rd 4 C3
Hillmay Rd 4 A4
Hitchens Clo 5 B2
Hobbs Hill Rd 8 C4
Hobletts Rd 6 C5
Hogg End La 7 G4
Hollybush La 5 B2
Home Park Mill Link Rd 10 D5
Homefield Rd 8 D1
Honeycross Rd 5 A4
Horsecroft Rd 5 C5
Horselers 8 D4
Horton Gdns 6 D1
Housewood End 5 C1
Howards Dri 5 B1
Howe Rd 8 D3
Hunters Oak 7 E2
Hunting Gate 6 B3
Huntsmill Rd 5 A5
Hyburn Clo 9 E2
Hyde La 10 D1
Hyperion Ct 6 D3

Innes Ct 4 D6
INDUSTRIAL ESTATES:
Doolittle Meadows
  Bus. Pk 8 C6
Happy Valley
  Ind Pk 10 D3

Home Park Ind Est 10 D5
Kings Park Ind Est 10 D3
Maxted Rd Ind Est 7 E4
Progression Centre 7 E4
Saracen Centre 7 E5
The Campus 7 E5
The Willows 7 E4
West Side 8 C6
Ionian Way 6 C4
Isenburg Way 6 B2
Iveagh Ct 4 C1

Jane Clo 7 F1
Jarman Clo 8 B3
Jennings Way 8 C3
Jocketts Hill 5 A4
Jocketts Rd 5 A4
Johnson Ct 8 B3
Juniper Grn 5 A3
Juno Rd 6 C4
Jupiter Dri 6 C5

Katrine Sq 6 B2
Keats Clo 7 E1
Keiths Rd 8 D2
Kendale 9 E2
Kents Av 8 B5
Kilbridge Ct 6 C2
Kiln Ground 8 D3
Kilncroft 9 E2
Kimps Way 8 D3
Kimpton Clo 7 E2
Kinder Scout 8 D2
King Edward St 8 A4
King Harry St 4 C3
Kingfisher Lure 10 D3
Kings Av 8 C5
Kings Meadow 10 D3
Kings Mews 6 A5
Kingsland Rd 5 C6
Kipling Gro 7 E1
Knights Orchard 5 A1
Knightsbridge Way 6 C6

Ladymeadow 10 A1
Laidon Sq 6 B2
Lamsey Rd 4 D5
Langdale 6 C3
Langley Av 8 C3
Langley Cres 10 D4
Langley Hill 10 B4
Langley Hill Clo 10 C4
Langley Lodge La 10 B6
Lapwing Clo 6 C3
Larchwood Rd 6 D4
Latimer Clo 7 E1
Laureate Way 5 C2
Laurel Clo 6 C6
Lavender Walk 6 A5
Lawn La 4 C5
Layhill 6 B4
Leaside 9 F2
Legfield Ter 5 B3
Leighton Buzzard Rd 4 B1
Leven Way 6 B2
Leverstock Green Rd,
  Adeyfield 7 E6
Leverstock Green Rd,
  Leverstock Grn 9 F2
Leverstock Green Way 9 F1
Leys Rd 8 C3
Lime Walk 8 C3
Linden Glade 5 C4
Lindlings 5 A5
Link Rd 6 A4
Linsey Clo 8 D5
Lismore 9 F3
Little Catherells 5 A1
Little Hayes 10 C4
Little Mimms 6 B5
Little Rd 6 C5
Lockers Park La 4 A2
Lombardy Clo 9 G2
Lomond Rd 6 B2
London Rd, Apsley 8 A4
London Rd, Boxmoor 5 A6
Long Arrotts 5 C1
Long Chaulden 5 A3
Long John 8 C3
Long Mimms 6 B5
Longdean Pk 8 D5
Longfield 9 E2
Longlands 6 D6
Lonsdale 6 B4
Love La 10 B3
Lovel Clo 5 C4
Lower Adeyfield Rd 4 D1
Lower Barn 8 C4
Lower Emms 7 F2
Lower Sales 5 B5

Lower Yott 8 C1
Lucks Hill 5 A4
Lyne Way 5 A2

Maddox Rd 9 E1
Malmes Croft 9 F3
Malus Clo 7 E6
Malvern Way 6 C4
Manan Clo 9 F3
Manley Rd 6 C6
Manor Av 8 A4
Manorville Rd 8 A5
Manscroft Rd 5 C1
Maple Grn 5 A2
Marchmont Grn 6 B4
Mariner Way 8 D2
Mark Rd 7 E4
Market Oak La 8 D5
Marlborough Rise 6 B3
Marlins Turn 5 C1
Marlowes 4 C3
Marnham Rise 5 C2
Marriots Way 4 D5
Marston Clo 8 D2
Martian Av 6 B4
Martindale Rd 5 B2
Marwood Clo 10 C4
Masons Rd 7 E5
Maxted Clo 7 F4
Maxted Rd 7 E4
Mayflower Av 4 D2
Maylands Av 7 E4
Maynard Rd 4 C3
Meadow Road 8 D5
Meadow Way,
  Hemel Hempstead 5 B6
Meadow Way,
  Kings Langley 10 C4
Meadowbank 10 D4
Medway Rd 6 C1
Medwick Mews 7 E2
Melsted Rd 4 A2
Mendip Way 6 C4
Mercers 6 B5
Mercury Walk 6 C4
Merrow Dri 5 A3
Mersey Clo 6 C2
Micklefield Rd 9 F1
Micklem Dri 5 B2
Midalgo Ct 6 C4
Middlehill 5 A4
Middleknights Hill 5 B1
Midland Rd 4 C2
Mill Clo 8 D6
Mill La 10 C3
Mill St 8 A4
Millfield Walk 9 E3
Milton Dene 7 E1
Mimas Rd 6 D3
Minstrel Clo 5 C2
Missden Dri 9 F3
Montgomery Av 6 D6
Moor End Rd 4 C4
Moorland Rd 5 B6
Mount Clo 5 B4
Mountfield Rd 6 B6
Musk Hill 5 A4
Myrtle Grn 5 A3

Nash Grn 5 D6
Neptune Dri 6 C5
Nettlecroft 4 A4
New Park Dri 7 E6
Newell Rd 8 B4
Newfield La 6 C6
Newford Clo 7 E5
Newlands Rd 5 A3
Nicholas Way 6 D5
Nidderdale 6 C3
Ninian Rd 6 B1
Northaw Clo 7 E1
Northend 9 E3
Northridge Way 5 B4

Oak Clo 8 D5
Oak St 8 C5
Oakdene Rd 8 C5
Old Crabtree La 8 C2
Old Fishery La 5 B6
Old House Ct 6 C6
Old House Rd 6 C6
Old Maple 6 D1
Oldfield Rd 5 A5
Olive Taylor Ct 6 C2
Oliver Clo 8 C5
Oliver Rise 8 C5
Oliver Road 8 C5
Oram Pl 8 A4
Orchard Clo 6 D5
Orchard St 8 C5
Oronsay 9 E3

Osbourne Av 10 C2

Paddock Way 5 A3
Palace Clo 10 C4
Pallas Rd 6 C4
Pamela Av 8 C3
Pancake La 9 G2
Panxworth Rd 4 D5
Paradise 4 D4
Park Cres 7 F1
Park Hill Rd 4 A3
Park La 4 D4
Park Rd 4 B4
Parkwood Dri 5 B3
Paston Rd 6 B4
Patmore Link Rd 9 F1
Peartree Clo 5 C3
Peartree Rd 5 C3
Peascroft Rd 8 D3
Pelham Ct 9 F1
Pennine Way 6 C3
Penrose Ct 6 B2
Pentland 6 C4
Perry Grn 7 E1
Pescot Hill 5 C2
Peterlee Ct 6 C3
Phoebe Rd 6 D4
Piccotts End 6 A3
Piccotts End La 6 A3
Piccotts End Rd 6 A3
Pinecroft 8 C5
Pinetree Clo 4 D1
Pinewood Gdns 4 A2
Pixies Hill Cres 5 B5
Pixies Hill Rd 5 B5
Plantation Walk 5 C1
Pluto Rise 6 C5
Polehanger La 5 A2
Pond Rd 8 D5
Poppy Clo 5 A2
Poynders Hill 9 F1
Primrose Clo 5 A5
Primrose Hill 10 D3
Prince Park 5 B4
Princes Ct 5 D6
Pudding La 5 C2
Puller Rd 5 C5
Pulleys Clo 5 B3
Pulleys La 5 B3
Punch Bowl La 7 G3
Putters Croft 6 C1

Quantocks 6 C4
Quartermass Clo 5 C3
Quartermass Rd 5 C3
Queensway 4 C1
Quinces Croft 5 C2

Railway Ter 10 C2
Ramson Rise 5 A5
Randalls Ride 6 B5
Ranelagh Rd 9 E1
Rannock Walk 6 A1
Rant Meadow 8 D3
Ranworth Clo 4 D5
Rathlin 9 E3
Ravensdell 5 A3
Raybarn Rd 5 C1
Rectory La 10 C3
Red Lion La 8 D6
Redbourne Rd 6 D3
Reddings 8 D3
Redditch Ct 8 B2
Redwood Dri 8 B2
Reson Way 4 A5
Reynolds Clo 5 C2
Ribblesdale 6 C3
Rice Clo 6 D5
Ridge Lea 5 B4
Ridgeway Clo 8 C6
Ripley Way 5 A3
Risedale Clo 8 C3
Risedale Hill 8 C3
Risedale Rd 8 B3
Ritcroft Clo 9 E2
Ritcroft Dri 9 E1
Ritcroft St 9 E2
River Pk 5 C6
Riversend Rd 8 A4
Riverside Clo 10 D4
Robbs Clo 5 C1
Robe End 5 A2
Robin Hood Meadow 6 C2
Robins Rd 8 D3
Robinsfield 5 A2
Rockliffe Av 10 D4
Roman Gdns 10 D4
Roseheath 5 A3
Rosehill Ct 5 C5
Rosewood Ct 5 A2
Roughdown Av 5 C6

Roughdown Rd 5 C6
Roughdown Villas Rd 5 B6
Roundwood 10 A1
Rowcroft 5 A4
Royal Ct 8 B4
Roydon Ct 7 E1
Rucklers La 10 A2
Rumballs Clo 8 D4
Rumballs Rd 9 E4
Runcorn Cres 6 C2
Runham Rd 8 B3
Russell Pl 5 D6
Rutland Gdns 6 D5
Rycroft Clo 9 F1

Sacombe Rd 5 B2
Saddlers Walk 10 C4
Saffron La 5 C2
St Agnells Ct 6 D2
St Agnells La 6 D1
St Albans Hill 8 B4
St Albans Rd 4 C5
St Andrews Rd 8 A5
St Anthonys Av 9 E2
St Davids Clo 9 G2
St Georges Rd 8 A5
St Johns Rd 4 A5
St Margarets Way 9 F1
St Marys Rd 6 A5
St Michaels Av 9 E2
St Nicholas Mt 5 B4
St Pauls Rd 4 D1
Sandalls Spring 5 A1
Sanday Clo 9 F3
Sanders Clo 8 D4
Sanders Rd 8 D4
Sandmere Clo 8 D2
Sandridge Clo 6 D1
Sanfoin End 6 D4
Saracens Head 6 D5
Sarratt Av 6 D1
Sarum Pl 6 C3
Saturn Way 6 C4
Sawyers Way 6 D6
School Row 5 A4
Scriveners Clo 4 D3
Seaton Rd 4 D6
Sebright Rd 5 C5
Selden Hill 4 C5
Semphill Rd 8 B3
Severn Mead 6 B3
Seymour Cres 6 B6
Sharp Croft 6 B4
Sheepcote Rd 8 C1
Sheephouse Rd 8 C3
Shenley Rd 7 E1
Shepherds Grn 5 A5
Sheridan Clo 5 C4
Sherwood Pl 6 C2
Shrub Hill Rd 5 B4
Sidford Clo 5 B3
Silverthorn Dri 9 E5
Simmonds Rise 4 D5
Six Acres 8 D3
Sleddale 6 C3
Sleets End 5 C1
Slippers Hill 6 B5
Small Acre 5 B3
Smithfield 6 B4
Solway 6 C4
Someries Rd 5 B2
South Hill Rd 4 B3
Southernwood Clo 6 D5
Speedwell Clo 5 A5
Spencer Way 5 B1
Spring La 5 B2
Spring Way 7 E5
Springfield Rd 6 C5
Squires Ride 6 D1
Squirrel Chase 5 A2
Standring Rise 5 C6
Station App 5 C6
Station Rd,
  Hemel Hempstead 4 A6
Station Rd,
  Kings Langley 10 D4
Stevenage Rise 6 C2
Stonelea Rd 8 C4
Storey St 8 A4
Stornaway 9 E3
Stratford Way 5 D6
Stroma Clo 9 F3
Stronsay Clo 9 F3
Stuarts Clo 4 D6
Summer Ct 6 A5
Sun Sq 6 A5
Sundew Rd 5 A5
Sunmead Rd 6 A5
Sunnyhill Rd 4 A2
Sunrise Cres 8 C3
Swallowdale La 6 D4

Sweetbriar Clo 5 C1
Sylvan Clo 8 D2

Talbot Ct 4 D6
Tamar Gdns 6 D1
Tannisfield Dri 6 C5
Tannismore Clo 6 D5
Taransay 9 E3
Tattershall Dri 7 E1
Taverners 6 B5
Tedder Rd 6 D6
Teesdale 6 B4
Temple Mead 6 B5
Tenzing Rd 6 D6
Tethys Rd 6 D4
Tewin Rd 9 F1
Thames Av 6 D1
Thatchers Croft 6 C3
The Apple Orchard 6 C5
The Avenue 5 A2
The Bounce 6 A4
The Brackens 4 D1
The Chase 8 C2
The Coltsfoot 5 A5
The Conifers 5 B6
The Coppice 7 E5
The Copse 5 A2
The Crofters 9 E2
The Dart 6 D1
The Dee 6 D1
The Dells 9 E2
The Denes 8 C5
The Farthings 5 C4
The Flags 7 E6
The Foxgloves 5 A5
The Gables 6 A5
The Glades 5 A2
The Glebe 10 C3
The Glen 6 D1
The Grazings 6 D1
The Holt 8 C2
The Horseshoe 9 F2
The Lawns 5 A2
The Leas 8 D5
The Maltings 6 B5
The Meadows 5 A2
The Melings 7 E2
The Nap 10 C3
The Nokes 5 C1
The Orchard 10 C4
The Orchards 8 B4
The Pastures 5 A2
The Poplars 5 C5
The Queens Sq 6 D6
The Rowans 5 C3
The Shrubbery 5 A2
The Sidings 4 D2
The Sonnets 5 D2
The Square 4 C3
The Thistles 5 C2
The Wayside 9 F2
The Wye 6 D1
Thistle Clo 5 A5
Thistle Croft 4 A4
Thorncroft 9 E2
Three Cherrytrees La 7 E2
Three Corners 8 D3
Thumpers 6 B5
Tile Kiln Clo 9 F2
Tile Kiln Cres 9 E2
Tile Kiln La 9 E2
Tile Kiln Rd 8 D2
Timplings Row 5 C2
Tintagel Clo 6 B2
Tiree Clo 9 E3
Titan Rd 6 C4
Tollpit End 5 C1
Toms Croft 8 B1
Tooveys Mill Clo 10 D3
Torridge Walk 6 D1
Towers Rd 6 C5
Townsend 6 A4
Travalga Way 6 B2
Trebellan Dri 6 C5
Tremaine Gro 6 B2
Tresilian Sq 6 D1
Trinity Ct 9 G2
Trinity Mews 9 G2
Triton Way 6 C4
Tudor Hill 4 C4
Turners Hill 8 B1
Turnpike Grn 6 C2
Two Waters Rd 4 C6
Tylers Clo 10 B3
Typleden Clo 6 BB4

Ullswater Rd 9 F2
Underacres Clo 6 D5
Union Grn 6 B5
Union St 6 B5
Upper Barn 8 C4

Upper Sales 5 B5
Uranus Rd 6 C5

Valley Grn 7 E1
Valleyside 5 B3
Varney Clo 5 B3
Varney Rd 5 B3
Vauxhall Rd 8 D1
Vesta Rd 6 C4
Vicarage Clo 4 B5
Vicarage La 10 B4

Wadey Clo 8 D2
Walnut Gro 4 D3
Wareside 6 D1
Warmark Rd 5 A2
Warners End Rd 4 A2
Washington Av 6 B2
Water La 10 D4
Waterhouse St 4 C3
Waterside 10 D3
Waterside Ct 10 D4
Watling Clo 6 C3
Waveney 6 D2
Wellbury Ter 9 F1
Wellcroft 5 C2
Wellen Rise 8 C4
Wellswood Clo 7 E6
Welwyn Ct 6 C3
Wensleydale 6 C3
West Valley Rd 8 A5
Westerdale 6 B3
Westray 9 F3
Westridge Clo 5 B4
Westview Rise 4 D1
Westwick Clo 9 G2
Westwick Row 9 G1
Weymouth St 8 A4
Wharf Rd 5 C6
Wharfedale 6 B4
Wheatfield 6 B4
Wheelers La 8 B3
White Hart Dri 8 C1
White Hart Rd 8 D2
White Hill 5 B4
White Lion St 8 B4
Whitebroom Rd 5 A2
Whiteleaf Rd 8 A4
Whitestone Walk 5 B1
Whitlars Dri 10 C3
Whitmores Wood 7 E5
Widford Ter 6 D1
Widmore Dri 6 D4
William Ct 8 A5
Willow Edge 10 D3
Willow Way 5 C2
Winchdells 8 D3
Windermere Clo 9 F2
Winding Shot 5 C3
Windmill Rd 6 C6
Windsend Clo 6 D5
Windsor Ct 10 D4
Winifred Rd 8 A4
Wolsey Rd 4 C4
Wood Crescent 4 D5
Wood End Clo 7 F5
Wood Farm Rd 8 B1
Wood La 4 D4
Wood Lane End 7 E5
Wood View 5 D2
Woodfield Dri 9 G3
Woodfield Gdns 9 G3
Woodhall La 6 C5
Woodland Av 4 A3
Woodland Clo 4 A4
Woodland Pl 4 A4
Woodlands Rd 10 D1
Woodman Rd 4 D6
Woolmer Dri 9 F1
Wootton Dri 6 C2
Wrensfield 5 C4
Wroxham Av 4 D5

Yeomans Ride 6 D1
Yew Tree Ct 5 C6
York Clo 10 C4
Youngfield Rd 5 B3

WATFORD

Abbots Rd 11 E6
Acme Rd 14 C2
Acorn Pl 14 C1
Addiscombe Rd 16 B4
Addison Clo 27 G6
Addison Way 27 G6
Adhara Rd 27 G4
Admirals Ct 14 B2
Adrian Rd 11 G5

Ainsdale Rd 28 A2
Akers La 17 D4
Albans Vw 13 E3
Albany Clo 23 G3
Albert Rd Nth 16 B2
Albert Rd Sth 16 B3
Aldbury Clo 13 G5
Aldbury Dri 28 B6
Aldbury Rd 18 B5
Aldenham Rd 15 G6
Alder Walk 13 E4
Alexandra Rd 16 A2
All Saints Cres 13 G2
All Saints La 19 H4
Allard Cres 23 F5
Alpine Walk 23 H5
Altair Way 27 F3
Altham Rd 28 C6
Alva Way 28 B1
Anglesey Rd 28 A4
Anselm Rd 28 D6
Anson Walk 26 C3
Anthony Clo 22 A4
Anthus Mews 27 E6
Apollo Av 27 G4
Appletree Walk 13 E4
Aquarius Way 27 G4
Aquila Clo 27 G3
Arbroath Grn 27 G2
Arden Clo 23 H3
Ardross Av 27 F4
Armand Clo 14 B2
Armitage Clo 19 E2
Arnett Clo 18 C4
Arnett Way 18 C4
Arthur St 15 F5
Ascot Rd 20 D3
Ash Clo,
  Abbots Langley 12 A1
Ash Clo, Garston 13 E5
Ash Hill Clo 23 E4
Ash Tree Rd 13 E6
Ash Vale 24 A4
Ashbourne Sq 27 E5
Ashburnham Clo 27 G2
Ashburnham Dri 27 G2
Ashby Rd 14 C2
Ashdon Rd 15 F5
Ashfield Av 23 E3
Ashfields 12 C5
Ashford Grn 28 B5
Ashleys 18 B5
Ashlyn Clo 15 F6
Ashridge Dri 28 A4
Ashurst Clo 27 F6
Askew Rd 26 D1
Aspen Park Dri 13 E5
Astons Rd 26 C4
Atria Rd 27 G4
Avalon Clo 13 H2
Avenue Rise 22 D1
Avenue Ter 22 B3
Avior Dri 27 F3
Avon Clo 13 F4
Aykho St 16 B5

Baird Clo 23 C2
Baldwins La 20 A1
Ballater Clo 28 A2
Ballenger Ct 16 A2
Balmoral Rd 14 B1
Banbury St 16 A3
Barden Clo 25 C3
Barley Clo 23 C1
Barn Lea 18 C6
Barnhurst Path 28 A4
Barton Way 20 A3
Basing Rd 24 C1
Batchworth
  Heath Hill 26 B3
Batchworth Hill 25 D1
Batchworth La 26 C4
Bateman Rd 20 A4
Bay Tree Walk 14 B2
Bayhurst Dri 27 F5
Beacon Way 18 C5
Beamish Dri 23 F5
Beauchamp Gdns 18 C6
Beaulieu Clo 21 H6
Bedford Av 26 D2
Bedford Rd 26 D3
Bedford St 14 D2
Bedmond Grn 11 H2
Bedmond Rd 11 H1
Beech Rd 14 C1
Beechcroft Av 20 B4
Beechcroft Rd 22 B1
Beechen Gro 16 B2
Beechpark Way 14 A1
Beechwood Av 17 B2
Beechwood Rise 13 E6

Beeston Clo	28 B3	Buckingham Rd	14 D1
Beggars Bush La	20 D3	Bucknalls Clo	13 H2
Bekan Ct	13 F5	Bucknalls La	13 G2
Belfair Gdns	28 B4	Bucks Av	22 B3
Belfry Av	24 D6	Bullsland Gdns	17 B4
Belgrave Av	21 F3	Bullsland La	17 B4
Belgrave Dri	11 E2	Burchell Ct	23 F4
Bell Clo	11 H2	Burfield Rd	17 B3
Bell La	11 H2	Burley Clo	28 A4
Bellamy Clo	14 B3	Burton Av	16 A4
Bellevue La	23 G4	Burtons La	17 A3
Bellmont Wood Av	14 A3	Bury La	19 F6
Belmont Rd	22 B1	Bury Meadows	19 F6
Bendysh Rd	15 F5	Bushell Gro	23 F5
Bennett Clo	27 F6	Bushey Mill Cres	13 F6
Benskin Rd	16 A6	Bushey Mill La	14 D1
Benton Rd	28 B4	Bushy Grove Rd	15 F6
Berceau Walk	14 A3	Bushy Hall Dri	15 G6
Beresford Rd	18 B6	Bushy Hall Rd	15 F6
Berkeley Clo	12 C1	Butterwick	13 H6
Berks Hill	17 C3	Buttlehide	24 A4
Berry Av	13 E6	Buttsmead	26 C6
Berry Clo	18 D5	Buxton Path	28 A2
Berry Gro La	15 F2	By the Wood	28 B1
Berry La, Chorleywood Bottom	17 D4	Byron Av	15 E3
Berry La, Moneyhill	18 C5	Caldecote Gdns	23 H3
Berry La, Rickmansworth	19 E6	Caldecote La	23 H3
Berry Way	18 D5	Caldwell Rd	28 B3
Biddenham Turn	13 F5	California La	23 G5
Birch Ct	26 C5	Callowland Clo	14 C2
Birch Dri	24 A4	Cambridge Rd	16 C5
Birchmead	14 B2	Campion Clo	12 D3
Birch Tree Walk	14 B1	Cannon Rd	16 D6
Birdstal Grn	28 B3	Canopus Way	27 G3
Birkdale Gdns	28 B2	Canterbury Clo	27 F5
Birken Mews	26 C4	Canterbury Rd	16 B1
Bishops Av	27 E3	Canterbury Way	20 B1
Biskra	14 B3	Capel Rd	22 B2
Black Moor La	20 C3	Capell Av	17 C3
Blacketts Wood Dri	17 A3	Capell Rd	17 C3
Blackford Rd	28 B4	Capell Way	17 C3
Blackley La	14 A1	Capella Rd	27 F3
Blackmoor La	20 C3	Capelvere Walk	14 A3
Blackthorn Clo	13 E2	Caractacus Cottage Vw	21 F5
Blackwell Dri	21 H4	Caractacus Grn	21 E4
Blairhead Dri	27 H2	Caravan La	19 G5
Blenheim Clo	22 A4	Cardiff Rd	16 C6
Bognor Gdns	28 A4	Carew Rd	27 E5
Boundary Way	13 F2	Carisbrooke Av	15 E3
Bourne End Rd	27 E3	Carlton Pl	26 C4
Bournehall Av	22 D2	Caroline Pl	22 B2
Bournehall La	22 D2	Carpenders Av	28 C2
Bournehall Rd	22 D2	Carpenters Wood Dri	17 B2
Bovingdon Cres	13 G4	Cassio Rd	16 A3
Bowling Ct	21 F2	Cassiobridge Rd	20 D2
Bowmans Grn	13 G6	Cassiobury Ct	14 A4
Bowring Grn	28 A4	Cassiobury Dri	16 A3
Bradberry	24 A4	Cassiobury Park Av	14 A5
Bradford Rd	17 B5	Castano Ct	12 C1
Bradshaw Rd	14 D3	Castle Clo	23 E3
Braeside Clo	28 D6	Catsey La	23 F4
Bramble Clo	12 D4	Catsey Wood	23 F3
Bramleas	21 E2	Caxton Way	20 D5
Brampton Rd	27 G2	Cecil St	14 D2
Bramsham Gdns	28 B4	Cedar Dri	28 D6
Bramshott Way	27 G1	Cedar Rd	22 A3
Branley Gdns	28 A4	Cedar Wood Dri	13 E5
Breakspeare Clo	14 C2	Cedars Av	19 E6
Breakspeare Rd	12 B1	Cervantes Ct	27 F6
Brett Pl	14 C1	Chaffinch La	21 E5
Briar Rd	13 E4	Chalfont La, Chorleywood West	17 A3
Bridge Pl	22 A2	Chalfont La, West Hyde	24 A6
Bridge Rd	12 A3	Chalfont Rd	24 A3
Bridger Clo	13 G2	Chalk Hill	22 B2
Bridgewater Way	23 E3	Chalmers Ct	19 G4
Bridle La	19 E1	Chapel Clo	12 D3
Bridle Path	16 C1	Chapmans Yd	16 D5
Bridlington Rd	28 B2	Charlock Way	21 E4
Briery Field	18 B2	Chartwell Rd	27 F5
Brighton Rd	14 C2	Chelwood Clo	26 D6
Brightwell Rd	16 A6	Chenies Rd	18 A1
Brixton Rd	14 D3	Chenies Way	20 D5
Broadfield Ct	23 G5	Cherry Hill	18 D1
Broadfield La	21 G6	Cherry Hollow	12 C1
Broadmead Clo	28 C6	Cherry Tree La	17 C6
Brocklesbury Clo	16 D2	Cherry Tree Rd	13 E6
Bromboro Grn	28 A4	Cherrydale	21 E2
Bromet Clo	14 A2	Cherwell Clo	20 A3
Brookdene Av	21 G5	Chesham Ct	27 F5
Brookdene Dri	27 F5	Chesham Way	21 E4
Brooke Clo	23 F4	Chess Clo	19 E2
Brooke Way	23 F4	Chess Hill	19 E2
Brookside	21 G5	Chess La	19 E2
Broom Gro	14 B2	Chess Way	18 C1
Broomfield Rise	12 A2	Chessvale Rise	19 G4
Bruce Rd	14 D2	Chester Rd, Northwood	27 F6
Brush Rise	13 E6		
Brushwood Av	17 B2		

Chester Rd, Watford	16 A5	Cygnet Clo	26 C5
Chestnut Av	18 C3	Cypress Walk	13 E5
Chestnut Rise	23 E4	Dairy Way	11 H4
Chestnut Walk	14 C1	Darwin Gdns	28 A4
Cheviot Clo	23 F2	Davenham Av	27 F4
Chichester Way	13 H3	De Havilland Way	12 C2
Chilcott Rd	12 C6	De Vere Walk	14 A4
Chiltern Av	23 E2	Deacons Hill	21 H4
Chiltern Clo	23 E2	Deakin Clo	21 E5
Chiltern Dri	18 B5	Deans Clo	12 B2
Chilwell Gdns	28 A3	Dell Rd	14 C1
Chiswell Ct	14 D2	Dell Side	14 C1
Chorleywood Bottom	17 C3	Dellfield Clo	16 A1
Chorleywood Clo	19 E5	Dellmeadow	11 G5
Chorleywood Rd	18 C2	Dellwood Clo	18 D6
Church Clo	27 F6	Delta Gain	28 B2
Church La	18 C6	Dene Rd	26 D5
Church Rd, Northwood	27 F6	Denewood Clo	14 A1
Church Rd, Watford	14 C3	Denham Way	24 B6
Church St, Rickmansworth	19 F6	Denmark St	16 A1
Church St, Watford	16 C4	Derby Rd	16 D4
Church Walk	23 E3	Derwent Av	28 C5
Clapgate Rd	23 E2	Desmond Rd	12 C6
Clare Ct	27 E4	Devereux Dri	14 A2
Claremont Cres	20 B3	Devon Rd	15 E3
Clarence Clo	23 H4	Diamond Rd	14 C2
Clarendon Rd	16 C1	Dickinson Av	20 A4
Clarke Way	12 D5	Dickinson Sq	20 A4
Clarkfield	18 C6	Dog Kennel La	18 B2
Clarks Mead	23 F4	Doncaster Grn	28 A4
Clay La	23 H4	Dormans Clo	27 E6
Claybury	23 E3	Dorrofield Clo	20 C3
Clements Rd	17 D3	Douglas Av	15 F1
Clifton Rd	16 B5	Dove Pk, Chorleywood	17 B4
Clitheroe Gdns	28 B3	Dove Pk, Hatch End	28 D6
Clive Way	15 E3	Dover Way	20 C2
Closemead Clo	26 D5	Downalong	23 G5
Clyston Rd	21 F4	Downings Path	24 A4
Coates Dell	13 H3	Dowry Walk	14 A2
Coates Way	13 G2	Drayton Ford	24 C1
Cobb Grn	13 E2	Drysdale Clo	27 E6
Codicote Dri	13 G4	Ducks Hill Rd	26 C6
Colburn Av	28 C5	Dugdales	19 H2
Coldharbour La	23 E2	Duke St	16 C3
Cole Rd	14 C3	Dulwich Way	20 A3
Coles Grn	23 F4	Dumfries Clo	27 G2
College Rd	12 D1	Duncan Way	15 G4
Collyland	17 C2	Dunsmore Clo	23 F3
Colne Av, Mill End	24 D1	Dunsmore Way	23 F3
Colne Av, Watford	21 G4	Durban Rd East	16 A4
Colne Mead	24 D1	Durban Rd West	16 A4
Colne Way	15 F1	Durrants Dri	20 B1
Colonial Way	15 E3	Dwight Rd	20 C5
Combe Rd	21 E4	Earl St	16 C3
Comet Clo	12 D4	East Dri	13 E5
Common Gate Rd	17 D3	East La	11 H2
Common Rd, Bushey Heath	23 G6	Eastbury Av	27 E4
Common Rd, Chorleywood	17 C2	Eastbury Pl	27 F4
Compton Rd	28 C3	Eastbury Rd, Northwood	27 E5
Comyne Rd	12 C6	Eastbury Rd, The Rookery	21 G5
Coningesby Dri	14 A4	Eastfield Av	15 E3
Cooks Mead	23 E2	Eastglade	27 F4
Coombe Hill Rd	18 C5	Eastlea Av	15 F1
Coombe Rd	23 F3	Eastwick Cres	24 C1
Copeswood Rd	14 C3	Eaton Gate	26 C5
Copmans Wick	17 C3	Ebury App	19 E6
Coppermill La	24 B6	Ebury Clo	26 D4
Copse Wood Way	26 C6	Ebury Rd, Rickmansworth	19 E6
Copthorne Clo	19 H3	Ebury Rd, Watford	16 D3
Copthorne Rd	19 G4	Edgbaston Rd	27 H2
Cornfield Rd	23 E1	Edinburgh Av	18 C4
Cornwall Rd	28 D6	Edridge Clo	23 E2
Cotswold Av	23 F2	Edward Clo	12 C2
Cottage Clo	19 H4	Elder Ct	23 H5
Cottage Dri	18 B3	Elderberry Way	13 E5
Courtlands Clo	12 C5	Elfrida Rd	16 C6
Courtlands Dri	14 A1	Elgin Dri	27 C3
Cow La	13 F5	Elgood Av	27 G5
Cowper Ct	14 C1	Elizabeth Ct	14 B2
Crabtree Clo	23 E1	Ellesboro' Clo	28 A4
Cranfield Dri	13 H2	Ellwood Gdns	13 F4
Creaseys Clo	11 H5	Elm Av	22 B4
Cress End	18 C6	Elm Gro	14 C1
Crofters Rd	27 E3	Elm Way	18 D6
Cromer Rd	14 D2	Elmcote Way	19 H4
Cross Rd	22 B2	Elstree Rd	23 G4
Cross St	16 C3	Elton Pk	16 A1
Crossmead	21 G4	Embleton Pk	27 G2
Crowboro' Path	28 B3	Emmanuel Rd	27 F6
Crown Pass	16 D5	Empire Centre	14 D3
Crown Rise	13 F4	Erskine Clo	28 B2
Croxley Vw	20 D4	Essex La	12 B3
Cuffley Av	13 G4	Essex Rd	16 A2
Cullera Clo	27 F5	Estcourt Rd	16 C3
Culverden Rd	27 H2		
Curtis Clo	24 D1		

Euston Av 21 F3
Evans Av 12 D5
Evans Clo 20 A3
Evelyn Dri 28 B6
Exchange Rd 16 B4

Fair Clo 23 E3
Fairfield Av 28 A2
Fairfolds 13 H5
Fairhaven Cres 27 G2
Fairlawns 14 B2
Fairseat Clo 23 G6
Fairview Dri 12 C6
Falcon Clo 27 E6
Falcon Way 13 H4
Falconer Rd 22 D2
Falkirk Gdns 28 B4
Faraday Clo 20 D4
Farm Field 14 A2
Farm La 18 D2
Farm Rd 26 C4
Farm Way, Bushey 23 E1
Farm Way, Eastbury 27 F3
Farmers Clo 13 E3
Farraline Rd 16 B5
Farriers Ct 13 E2
Fay Grn 12 B3
Fearney Mead 18 C6
Fearnley St 16 B5
Federal Way 15 E3
Felden Clo, Garston 13 G4
Felden Clo, Hatch End 28 C6
Fern Way 13 E4
Ferndown Clo 28 C6
Ferndown Rd 28 A3
Fernhills 12 A3
Ferryhills Clo 28 B2
Fidler Pl 23 E3
Field End Clo 22 B3
Field Rd 22 B2
Field Way 18 D6
Fifth Av 13 G5
Finch La 22 D1
Finucane Rise 23 F5
Firbank Dri 22 B3
Firs Walk 26 D5
First Av 13 F5
Fleetwood Way 28 A3
Florence Clo 12 D4
Florida Clo 23 G5
Follett Dri 12 C1
Ford Clo 23 F1
Forest Rd 13 E3
Forest Walk 15 G3
Forge La 27 E6
Fotherley Rd 24 C1
Fourth Av 13 G5
Fox Clo 23 E1
Foxdell 27 E5
Foxfield Clo 27 F5
Foxgrove Path 28 B4
Foxhill 13 E6
Foxlands Clo 12 D4
Foxleys 28 C2
Francis Rd 16 B4
Frankland Clo 20 A4
Frankland Rd 20 A4
Franklin Rd 16 B2
Friars Way 15 G3
Frinton Clo 27 H1
Frithwood Av 27 E5
Frogmore La 25 G1
Fulford Gro 28 A1
Fuller Gdns 14 D1
Fuller Rd 14 C1
Fuller Way 20 A3
Furtherfield 12 C2
Furze Clo 28 A4
Furze Vw 17 C4

Gable End 12 B2
Gaddesden Cres 13 G4
Gade Av 20 D2
Gade Bank 20 D2
Gade Clo 21 E2
Gade Side 12 C5
Gade View Gdns 12 A2
Gadswell Clo 13 G6
Gallows Hill 12 A2
Gallows Hill La 12 A1
Gammons Farm Clo 12 C5
Gammons La 14 B1
Ganders Ash 12 D3
Ganton Walk 28 B3
Garden Clo 14 B4
Garden Rd 12 B1
Garfield St 14 C2

Garnet Clo 13 G6
Garratts Rd 23 F3
Garsmouth Way 13 G6
Garston Cres 13 F4
Garston Dri 13 F4
Garston La 13 G4
Garston Park Par 13 G4
Gartlet Rd 16 C3
Gate End 27 E6
Gatehill Rd 27 F6
Gateway Clo 26 C5
Gaumont App 16 B3
Gazelda Villas 22 A2
Geddes Rd 23 F1
George St 16 C4
Georges Dri 28 C2
Giant Tree Hill 23 F5
Gibbs Couch 28 B2
Gillian Clo 23 F5
Girtin Rd 23 E1
Girton Way 20 B3
Gladstone Rd 16 D3
Gleed Av 23 F5
Glen Way 14 A2
Glencoe Rd 22 D2
Gleneagles Clo 28 B4
Glengorse Grn 28 B3
Glenmore Gdns 12 D1
Goldcrest Way 23 F4
Golf Clo 15 F5
Gonville Av 20 A4
Goodrich Clo 12 D5
Goodwood Av 12 B5
Goodwood Par 12 C6
Goral Mead 19 F6
Gorle Clo 12 D4
Gosforth La 28 A2
Gosforth Path 27 G2
Grandfield Av 14 B3
Grange Rd 22 B2
Granville Rd 16 C5
Grasmere Clo 13 E2
Great Gro 23 E1
Greatham Rd 15 F5
Green La, Northwood 26 D5
Green La, Rickmansworth 19 H3
Green La, Watford Hth 21 H5
Green St 17 C1
Greenacres 23 G5
Greenbank Rd 12 B5
Greenbury Clo 17 C2
Greenfield Av 28 B1
Greenhall Cres 20 A4
Greenhills Clo 18 C3
Greensward 23 E3
Greenways 12 B1
Greenwood Clo 23 G4
Greenwood Dri 13 E4
Greycaine Rd 15 E1
Grimsdyke Rd 28 C6
Grosvenor Avenue 11 E2
Grosvenor Rd, Eastbury 27 F4
Grosvenor Rd, Watford 16 D4
Grove Cres 20 A2
Grove Farm Pk 26 D4
Grove Rd, Moneyhill 24 D1
Grove Rd, Moor Park 26 D4
Grove Way 17 B3
Grovehall Rd 15 F6
Grover Rd 22 B3
Grovewood Clo 17 A2
Guland Clo 23 E1
Gulletwood Rd 13 E4
Gwent Clo 13 G4
Gypsy La 12 A5

Haddon Rd 17 B3
Hagden La 16 A6
Haines Way 12 D3
Halifax Rd 17 C5
Hall Clo 18 C6
Hall Dri 25 F6
Hallam Gdns 28 C6
Halland Way 26 D5
Hallowell Rd 27 E6
Hallowes Cres 27 G2
Halsey Pl 14 D2
Halsey Rd 16 B3
Hamilton Clo 23 H6
Hamilton Rd, Abbots Langley 12 A2
Hamilton Rd, South Oxhey 27 H2
Hamilton St 16 D6
Hampden Way 12 B6
Hampermill La 21 F6

Handsworth Clo 27 G2
Hanger Ruding 28 D2
Harborne Clo 28 A4
Harcourt Rd 23 E2
Harding Clo 13 F3
Hare Cres 13 E2
Harefield Rd 25 G1
Harewood 18 D3
Harewood Rd 28 A2
Harford Dri 14 A2
Harriet Way 23 G4
Harris Rd 12 D5
Harrison Clo 26 D5
Harrogate Rd 28 A2
Harrow Way 28 C2
Harthall La 11 E2
Harts Clo 15 H3
Hartsbourne Av 23 F6
Hartsbourne Clo 23 G6
Hartsbourne Rd 23 G5
Hartspring La 15 H4
Harvest End 13 G6
Harvest Rd 23 E1
Harvey Rd 20 A4
Harwoods Rd 16 A5
Hastings Way, Croxley Green 20 B2
Hastings Way, Watford 15 F6
Hatfield Rd 14 D3
Hatters La 20 C4
Hawes Clo 27 F6
Hawksworth Clo 27 E6
Heather Clo, Abbots Langley 12 D1
Hawthorn Clo, Watford 14 B2
Hawthorns 24 A4
Haydon Rd 22 B2
Hayfield Clo 23 E1
Hayling Rd 27 F2
Haywood Park 18 B3
Hazel Gro 13 E5
Hazel Tree Rd 13 E6
Hazelbury Av 12 A2
Hazelwood Rd 20 B4
Hazelwood La 12 A2
Healey Rd 21 E4
Heath Rd 22 B3
Heathbourne Rd 23 H5
Heather Clo 12 D2
Heather Rise 15 H4
Heathfield Rd 22 C1
Heathside Clo 26 D4
Heathside Rd 26 D3
Hedgeside Rd 26 C4
Helston Pl 12 C2
Hemingford Rd 12 B6
Hemming Way 12 D5
Hempstead Rd 14 A1
Henbury Way 28 B2
Henderson Pl 11 H2
Herga Ct 16 A1
Herkomer Clo 23 E3
Herkomer Rd 22 D2
Herne Rd 23 E2
Heron Clo 25 G1
Heron Walk 27 F3
Herons Lea 13 F5
Heronsgate Rd 17 B4
Heswell Grn 27 G2
Heysham Dri 28 A4
Hibbert Av 15 E2
High Acres 12 A2
High Clo 18 D3
High Elms Clo 26 D5
High Elms La 13 F1
High Rd, Bushey Heath 23 G5
High Rd, Leavesden Green 12 C5
High St, Abbots Langley 11 G5
High St, Bedmond 11 H3
High St, Bushey 22 D2
High St, Northwood 27 F6
High St, Rickmansworth 19 E6
High St, Watford 16 B3
High Vw, Chorleywood 18 C2
High Vw, Watford 21 E4
Highfield Rd 22 B2
Highfield Way 18 C4
Highland Dri 23 E3
Highlands 21 H6
Highwood Av 15 G3
Hilfield La 23 G1
Hilfield La Sth 23 G2
Hill End Rd 25 E5
Hill Farm Av 12 D2
Hill Farm Clo 12 D3

Hill Rise 18 D4
Hill Road 26 D5
Hill Ter 12 D2
Hillard Rd 27 F6
Hillcroft Cres 21 G6
Hillingdon Rd 13 E4
Hillrise Av 15 F2
Hillsborough Grn 27 G2
Hillside Clo 12 B2
Hillside Cres 22 B3
Hillside Gdns 27 G6
Hillside Rise 27 G6
Hillside Rd, Bushey 22 B2
Hillside Rd, Chorleywood 17 C3
Hillside Rd, Northwood 27 G6
Hilltop Rd 11 F2
Hillview Clo 28 D5
Hillview Rd 28 D6
Hindhead Grn 28 A4
Hive Clo 23 G5
Hive Rd 23 G5
Holbein Gate 27 F4
Holland Gdns 13 F5
Hollybush Clo 21 H5
Hollygrove 23 G4
Holmbury Clo 23 G6
Holme Lea 13 F4
Holmside Rise 27 H2
Holtsmere Clo 13 F5
Holywell Rd 16 A6
Home Farm Road 26 A3
Home Way 18 B6
Homefield Rd, Bushey 22 D1
Homefield Rd, Chorleywood 17 C2
Homestead Rd 19 F5
Hope Grn 12 D2
Hornhill Rd 24 A4
Horseshoe La 13 E1
Horsleys 24 A4
Howard Clo, Little Bushey 23 H4
Howard Clo, Watford 14 B1
Howton Pl 23 G5
Hoylake Gdns 28 B3
Hubbards Rd 17 C3
Hudson Clo 12 C5
Huntercombe Gdns 28 A4
Hunters La 12 D3
Huntonbridge Hill 12 A3
Hyde La 11 E1
Hyde Rd 16 A2

Ilkley Rd 28 B4
Imperial Way 15 E3
INDUSTRIAL ESTATES:
Cardiff Rd Ind Est 21 G3
Croxley Bus. Park 20 D3
Greatham Rd Ind Est 15 E5
Greycaine Ind Est 13 F6
Maple Cross Ind Est 24 C3
Metro Centre 20 C5
Moor Park Ind Centre 20 C5
Otterspool Way Ind Est 15 H3
Vale Ind Park 20 B6
Watford Bus. Park 20 C4
West Watford Bus. Centre 21 E4
Wolsey Bus. Park 20 C5
Woodcock Hill Trading Est 25 G3
Ivinghoe Clo 13 G5
Ivinghoe Rd, Bushey 23 F3
Ivinghoe Rd, Mill End 18 B5

Jackets La 26 A6
Jacketts Field 11 H5
James Clo 22 B1
Jordan Clo 12 C4
Jubilee Rd 14 C2
Judge St 14 C2
Juniper Clo 25 G2
Juniper Gate 25 G2
Juniper Gro 14 B2

Keble Ter 12 C1
Kelmscott Clo 21 F3
Kelmscott Cres 21 F3
Kelshall 13 H6
Kemp Pl 22 D3
Kemps Dri 27 F6
Kenford Clo 13 E2
Kenilworth Ct 14 B3
Kenilworth Dri 20 A2
Kenilworth Gdns 28 A4

Kennedy Clo 28 D5
Kensington Av 21 F2
Kenwood Dri 24 C1
Keston Mews 16 B1
Kestrel Clo 13 H4
Kewferry Dri 26 C4
Kewferry Rd 26 D5
Kilby Clo 13 G4
Kildonan Clo 14 B3
Kilmarnock Rd 28 B3
Kiln Way 27 E5
Kimble Clo 21 E4
Kimble Cres 23 F3
Kimpton Pl 13 G4
Kindersley Way 11 E6
King Edward Rd 22 B2
King George Av 23 E3
King Georges Av 21 E2
King St 16 C5
Kingfisher Lure 18 D2
Kings Av 21 F2
Kings Clo, Northwood 27 F5
Kings Clo, Watford 16 C5
Kings Farm 17 C4
Kingsfield Ct 22 A3
Kingsfield Rd 22 A3
Kingswood Rd 13 E4
Kirby Clo 27 F5
Kirkcaldy Grn 28 A2
Knutsford Av 15 E2
Koh-i-Noor Av 22 D2
Kytes Dri 13 G3

Ladys Clo 16 C5
Ladywalk 24 B4
Ladywood Clo 18 D1
Lake Dri 23 F6
Lamb Clo 13 F5
Lambert Ct 15 F6
Lammas Rd 16 C6
Lancaster Way 12 C1
Lancing Way 20 B3
Landford Clo 25 G1
Lane Gdns 23 H4
Langholme 23 F4
Langland Ct 26 D6
Langland Dri 28 C6
Langley La 12 D1
Langley Rd,
 Abbots Langley 11 G5
Langley Rd, Watford 16 A1
Langley Way 14 A4
Langmead Dri 23 G4
Langton Gro 26 D4
Langwood Gdns 14 C3
Lansdowne Clo 13 G4
Larken Dri 23 F4
Latimer Clo 20 D5
Lauderdale Rd 12 A2
Laurino Pl 23 F6
Lavinia Av 13 G4
Lavrock La 19 G5
Lawford Av 17 B4
Lawford Clo 17 B4
Lea Bushes 13 G5
Lea Clo 23 E1
Leaf Clo 27 E6
Leaford Cres 14 B1
Leander Gdns 15 F1
Leavesden Rd 14 C2
Lebanon Clo 12 B6
Leeway Clo 28 C6
Leggatts Clo 12 D5
Leggatts Rise 12 D5
Leggatts Way 12 D5
Leggatts Wood Av 13 E6
Leigh Rd 28 C2
Lemonfield Dri 13 H2
Letchworth Clo 28 B5
Leven Clo 28 B4
Leveret Clo 12 D4
Lewes Way 20 B2
Lime Clo 22 B3
Lime Tree Walk 18 D3
Limetree Walk 23 H5
Lincoln Dri,
 Croxley Green 20 B2
Lincoln Dri,
 Sth Oxhey 28 A2
Lincoln Way 20 A2
Linden Lea 12 D3
Lingfield Clo 27 E6
Link Rd 15 E4
Links Way,
 Croxley Green 20 C2
Links Way,
 Moor Park 26 D6
Linnet Clo 23 F4
Liphook Rd 28 B3
Little Bushey La 23 F1
Little Graylings 12 B2

Little Green La 20 A1
Little Gro 23 E1
Little Hill 17 C4
Little How Croft 11 E6
Little Martins 23 E1
Little Orchard Clo 12 B1
Little Oxhey La 28 B4
Little Potters 23 G4
Little Stream Clo 27 E4
Liverpool Rd 16 B6
Loates La 16 C3
Local Board Rd 16 D6
Lodge Dri 19 E2
Lodge End 20 C1
London Rd, Bushey 22 C2
London Rd,
 Moor Park 26 A3
Long Barn Clo 13 E2
Long Croft 21 G5
Long Croft Rd 24 A4
Long Elms 12 A3
Long Elms Clo 12 A3
Long La,
 Chorleywood 17 B4
Long La, Mill End 24 C1
Longcliffe Path 27 G2
Longlees 24 A4
Longmore Clo 24 C3
Longspring 14 C1
Lorane Ct 16 A1
Lord St 16 C3
Loudwater Dri 19 E2
Loudwater Heights 18 D1
Loudwater La 19 E3
Loudwater Ridge 19 E2
Louvain Way 13 E2
Lovatts 20 A2
Love La,
 Abbots Langley 11 H4
Lower High St 22 A1
Lower Paddock Rd 22 B2
Lower Plantation 19 E1
Lower Rd 17 C2
Lower Tail 28 C2
Lower Tub 23 G3
Lowestoft Rd 14 D3
Lowson Gro 22 B4
Ludlow Mead 27 H2
Ludlow Way 20 C2
Lundin Walk 28 B3
Lych Gate 13 G3
Lyndon Av 28 C5
Lynwood Heights 18 D3
Lytham Av 28 B4

Macdonnell Gdns 12 C5
McKellar Clo 23 F5
Magnaville Rd 23 H4
Magnolia Av 12 D1
Magpie Hall Rd 23 H5
Main Av 26 C2
Main Par 17 C2
Malden Rd 16 A1
Mallard Way,
 Meriden 13 H6
Mallard Way,
 Moor Park 26 C6
Malvern Way 20 B3
Mandela Pl 16 D2
Manderville Clo 14 B2
Manor House Dri 26 C6
Manor House Gdns 11 F6
Manor Rd 14 C3
Manor Way 20 A2
Maple Clo 15 F4
Maple Gro 14 C3
Maple Leaf Clo 12 D2
Maplelodge Clo 24 B3
Margarets Clo 12 C2
Marge Holes 28 C1
Marion Clo 15 G3
Markab Rd 27 G4
Markeston Grn 28 B3
Market Pl 16 C4
Market St 16 B4
Marlborough Rd 16 B4
Marlin Sq 12 C1
Marlins Meadow 20 D4
Marsworth Av 28 B6
Marsworth Clo 20 D5
Matlock Cres 28 A2
Maude Cres 14 D2
Maxwell Clo 24 D1
Maxwell Rise 22 B3
Maxwell Road 27 E6
Maycock Gro 27 F5
Mayfare 20 C3
Maylands Rd 28 A3
Maythorne Clo 20 D2
Maytree Cres 12 C5
Mead Pl 18 D6

Mead Way 15 F4
Meadow Rd,
 Bushey Heath 23 E1
Meadow Rd, Garston 13 E4
Meadow Way,
 Bedmond 11 H2
Meadow Way,
 Rickmansworth 19 E5
Meadowbank 21 H5
Meadowcroft 23 E3
Medway Clo 13 F4
Melbourne Rd 23 E2
Melrose Pl 14 B2
Mendip Rd 23 F2
Meredith Clo 28 B6
Meriden Way 13 H6
Merrows Clo 26 C5
Merry Hill Mount 23 E4
Merry Hill Rd 23 H4
Merton Rd 16 B5
Mezen Clo 26 D4
Middle Furlong 23 E1
Middle Rope 14 C1
Middle Way 14 C1
Middleton Rd 18 C6
Mildred Av 16 A4
Mill Way, Mill End 18 B6
Mill Way, Watford 15 F4
Millbrook Rd 15 G3
Millhouse La 11 H2
Millthorn Clo 19 G3
Milner Ct, Bushey 23 E3
Milner Ct,
 Kingswood 13 E3
Milton St 14 C2
Minerva Dri 12 B5
Moat Clo 23 E2
Moatfield Rd 23 E1
Moatview Ct 23 E2
Molteno Rd 14 B3
Money Hill Rd 18 D6
Monica Clo 16 D1
Monmouth Rd 16 B2
Montacute Rd 23 H3
Moor La 20 B6
Moor Lane Crossing 20 C5
Moor Park Rd 26 D4
Moor Vw 21 F4
Moortown Rd 28 A3
Morgan Clo 27 F5
Morriston Clo 28 A4
Mortimer Clo 23 E3
Moss Clo 25 G1
Moss Rd 13 E4
Mostyn Rd 23 F1
Mount Vw,
 Moneyhill 18 D6
Mount Vw,
 Northwood 27 G5
Muirfield Clo 28 A4
Muirfield Grn 28 A3
Muirfield Rd 28 A3
Mullion Walk 28 B3
Munden Dri 15 G1
Munden Gro 15 E2
Mundesly Clo 28 A3
Mungo Park Clo 23 F5
Munro Rd 23 E1
Muriel Av 16 D6
Murray Rd 27 E6
Mutchetts Clo 13 H3
Myrtleside Clo 26 D6

Nairn Grn 27 G2
Nancy Downs 22 A4
Napier Dri 15 F6
Nascot Pl 16 B1
Nascot Rd 16 B1
Nascot St 16 B1
Nascot Wood Rd 14 A1
Neal St 16 C6
Neston Rd 14 D1
Nevill Gro 14 D2
Nevill Clo 28 A3
New Biggin Path 28 A3
New Rd,
 Croxley Green 20 A3
New Rd, Watford 16 D5
New St 16 C4
Newhouse Cres 13 E2
Newland Clo 28 C5
Newlands Walk 13 G3
Newport Mead 28 B3
Newquay Gdns 28 A1
Nicholas Clo 14 D1
Nicholson Dri 23 F5
Nightingale Pl 19 E5
Nightingale Rd,
 Bushey 22 D2
Nightingale Rd,
 Rickmansworth 19 E5
Nimmo Dri 23 G4

Norbury Av 16 D1
Norfolk Av 15 E2
Norfolk Rd 19 F6
Normans Field Clo 23 E3
North App,
 Leavesden Green 12 D5
North App,
 Moor Park 26 D1
North Orbital Rd 12 C5
North Rd 17 C3
North Western Av 12 B5
North Western Av
 (Colne Way) 15 F1
North Western Av
 (Tylers Way) 23 G1
Northbrook Dri 27 E6
Northfield Gdns 15 E1
Northgate 26 C6
Northway 19 F5
Northwick Rd 28 A3
Northwood Rd 25 G6
Northwood Way 27 G6
Norwich Way 20 B1
Nottingham Clo 12 D3
Nottingham Rd 17 C5
Nuttfield Clo 20 B4

Oak Green 12 C1
Oak Green Way 12 C1
Oak Path 23 E3
Oakdale Clo 28 A3
Oakdale Rd 28 A3
Oakdene Clo 28 D6
Oakdene Rd 13 E6
Oakfield 18 B5
Oakhill Rd 24 A3
Oaklands Av 21 G6
Oaklands Ct 14 B3
Oaklands Gate 27 E5
Oakleigh Dri 20 B4
Oakleigh Rd 28 D5
Occupation Rd 16 B6
Old Barn La 19 H3
Old Forge Clo 12 D2
Old Gannon Clo 26 C3
Old Mill Rd 12 A3
Old Shire La 17 A5
Old Uxbridge Rd 24 B4
Olds App 20 B5
Olds Clo 20 B5
On the Hill 28 C1
Orbital Cres 12 D5
Orchard Av 13 E1
Orchard Clo,
 Chorleywood 17 C2
Orchard Clo,
 Little Bushey 23 G4
Orchard Clo,
 Watford 14 B3
Orchard Dri,
 Chorleywood 17 C1
Orchard Dri,
 Watford 14 B3
Orchard Way 18 C5
Orion Way 27 F3
Ormonde Rd 26 D3
Ormskirk Rd 28 B4
Orphanage Rd 16 C2
Orwell Ct 16 D2
Osborne Rd 14 D2
Osprey Clo 13 H4
Otley Way 28 A2
Otterspool La 15 G2
Otterspool Way 15 G2
Otterspool Way
 Service Rd 15 H3
Ottoman Ter 16 D3
Oulton Way 28 C3
Oundle Av 23 F2
Overstream 18 D2
Owens Way 20 A2
Oxford St 16 B6
Oxhey Dri 27 H4
Oxhey Drive Sth 27 H4
Oxhey La 28 D1
Oxhey Ridge Clo 27 H4
Oxhey Road 22 B4

Palmer Av 23 E2
Pankhurst Pl 16 D2
Park Av, Bushey 15 F4
Park Av,
 Rickmansworth 18 C3
Park Av, Watford 16 A4
Park Clo,
 Moor Park 26 B3
Park Clo, Watford 15 C3
Park La 24 D6
Park Par 28 D6
Park Rd, Bushey 22 D2

Park Rd, Rickmansworth	19 F5
Park Rd, Watford	14 C3
Park Side Rd	27 F4
Park Vw	28 D6
Park View Rd	27 H5
Park Way	18 D6
Parker St	14 C3
Parkfield	18 B2
Parkgate Rd	14 D1
Parkside	22 A3
Parkside Dri	14 A4
Parnell Clo	11 H4
Parrots Clo	19 H2
Parsonage Clo	11 G4
Parsonage La	19 E5
Partridge Clo	23 E4
Pasture Clo	23 F3
Paynestield Rd	23 H4
Pembroke Rd	26 C2
Penn Clo	17 C4
Penn Rd, Mill End	24 D1
Penn Rd, Watford	14 D3
Penn Way	17 C4
Penrose Av	28 C1
Pentland Rd	23 F2
Percy Rd	16 B4
Peregrine Clo	13 H4
Perivale Gdns	13 E4
Perrymead	23 E3
Pheasants Way	18 C5
Phillipers	13 G5
Phoenix Way	27 G3
Pickets Clo	23 G4
Piggy La	17 A4
Pilgrims Clo	13 G2
Piltdown Rd	28 B3
Pinchfield	24 B4
Pine Gro	15 G4
Pinehurst Clo	12 B2
Pines Clo	27 F5
Pinfold Rd	15 G4
Pinner Hill	28 A6
Pinner Rd	22 B2
Plaitford Clo	25 G1
Plough La	25 E5
Police Station La	23 E4
Pollards	24 A4
Pomeroy Cres	13 E6
Popes La	14 C1
Popes Rd	12 B1
Poplars Clo	13 E2
Potter Heights Clo	27 H6
Potter Street Hill	27 H5
Pound Field	12 C5
Prestwick Rd	28 B1
Pretoria Rd	16 A5
Primrose Gdns	23 E4
Prince St	16 C3
Princes Av	14 B6
Priory Vw	23 G4
Prowse Av	23 F5
Pryor Clo	12 C1
Purbrock Av	13 F5
Purlings Rd	23 E1
Puttenham Clo	28 B2
Queen Marys Av	14 A6
Queens Av	14 B6
Queens Dri	12 C1
Queens Pl	16 D3
Queens Rd	16 C2
Queens Wood Cres	13 E3
Quickley Brow	17 B4
Quickley La	17 B4
Quickley Rise	17 B4
Quickwood Clo	18 B4
Radlett Rd	16 D3
Raglan Gdns	21 G6
Railway Cotts	14 D3
Rainbow Ct	21 H4
Ralston Way	28 B1
Ransome Clo	21 H5
Raphael Dri	16 D2
Rasehill Clo	18 D3
Raven Clo	19 E5
Ravenscroft	13 H4
Ravenswood Pk	27 G5
Raymond Clo	12 A2
Rectory La	19 E6
Rectory Rd	19 E6
Reddings Av	23 E2
Redheath Clo	12 D4
Redwood Clo	28 B3
Reeds Cres	16 C1
Regal Way	15 E2
Regent St	14 D2
Regents Ct	12 C2
Reginald Rd	27 F6
Rendlesham Way	17 C4
Repton Way	20 A3
Rhodes Way	15 E3
Richards Clo	23 G4
Richfield Rd	23 F4
Richmond Dri	14 A4
Richmond Way	20 C2
Rickmansworth By-Pass	19 F5
Rickmansworth Rd, Chorleywood	18 A1
Rickmansworth Rd, Hill End	25 F6
Rickmansworth Rd, Northwood	26 C5
Rickmansworth Rd, Watford	14 A6
Ridge La	14 A1
Ridge St	14 D2
Ridge Way	18 D5
Ridgehurst Av	12 D3
Rising Hill Clo	26 C5
Risingholme Clo	23 E3
Riverside Dri	19 E6
Riverside Rd	21 G4
Roberts Rd	16 C6
Robin Hood Dri	15 G3
Robinson Cres	23 F5
Rochester Way	20 A2
Rofant Rd	27 E5
Romilly Dri	28 C3
Rooks Hill	19 E2
Rose Gdns	21 F3
Rose Lawn	23 F5
Roseberry Ct	14 B3
Rosebery Rd	23 E4
Rosebriar Walk	12 C6
Rosecroft Dri	12 B6
Rosehill Gdns	12 A2
Ross Cres	12 D4
Ross Way	27 F3
Rosslyn Rd	16 B3
Rossway Dri	23 F2
Rother Clo	13 F4
Roughwood Clo	14 A2
Rounton Dri	14 B2
Rousebarn La	20 B1
Rowley Clo	22 B2
Roy Rd	27 F6
Royston Gro	28 D5
Royston Park Rd	28 D5
Rudolph Rd	22 D2
Rugby Way	20 A3
Rushmore Clo	25 G1
Rushton Av	12 D5
Russell Clo	26 D4
Russell Cres	12 C5
Russell La	12 A5
Russell Rd	26 D4
Rutherford Way	23 G5
Rutland Pl	23 G4
Ryan Way	15 E3
Rydal Ct	13 E2
Ryder Clo	23 E2
Ryman Ct	17 C4
St Albans La	11 H1
St Albans Rd, Garston	13 F5
St Albans Rd, Kyte	13 G1
St Albans Rd, Watford	16 B2
St Andrews Prec	28 B2
St Annes Clo	28 A3
St Cuthbert Gdns	28 D5
St Francis Clo	21 G6
St Georges Rd	14 D2
St James's Rd	16 B5
St Johns Rd	16 B2
St Lawrence Clo	11 G5
St Leonards Clo	15 F6
St Martins Clo	28 A3
St Marys Av	27 E4
St Marys Rd	16 B5
St Matthews Clo	22 A2
St Pauls Way	16 D2
St Peters Clo, Little Bushey	23 G4
St Peters Clo, Moneyhill	18 D6
St Peters Way	17 A2
Salisbury Rd	14 D2
Salter Gdns	14 C3
Sanctuary Clo	25 F6
Sandown Rd	14 D2
Sandringham Rd	14 D1
Sandy La	27 F1
Sandy Lodge La	26 D1
Sandy Lodge Rd	26 B1
Sandy Lodge Way	27 E4
Sarratt La	18 D1
Sarratt Rd	19 G1
School La	23 E4
School Mead	12 B2
Scot Grove	28 B6
Scots Hill	19 G4
Scots Hill Clo	19 H4
Scots Mill La	19 G4
Scottswood Clo	15 G4
Scottswood Rd	15 F4
Seabrook Rd	11 F2
Seacroft Gdns	28 B3
Second Av	13 G5
Sequoia Clo	23 G5
Sergehill La	11 H1
Seven Acres	27 G5
Severn Way	13 F4
Shady Bush Clo	23 F4
Shady La	16 B2
Shaftesbury Rd	16 D3
Shaftesbury Way	11 E2
Shakespeare St	14 C2
Shanklin Gdns	28 A3
Shaw Clo	23 G5
Sheepcot Dri	13 F4
Sheepcot La	12 D3
Shefton Rise	27 G6
Shelley Clo	27 F4
Shephards Walk	23 G5
Shepherds La	17 C4
Shepherds Rd	21 E1
Shepherds Way	18 D5
Sheppeys La	11 F3
Sheraton Mews	20 D2
Sherborne Way	20 A2
Sherfield Av	25 G2
Sheridan Rd	22 A4
Sheriff Way	12 D3
Sherwoods Rd	22 B4
Shire La	17 B3
Shirley Rd	12 C2
Shrubs Rd	25 G4
Sidmouth Clo	27 H1
Silk Mill Ct	21 G5
Silk Mill Rd	21 G5
Silver Dell	12 C5
Silverdale Rd	22 B1
Simon Ct	22 D2
Sirus Rd	27 G4
Siskin Clo	15 F6
Sixth Av	13 G4
Skidmore Way	19 F6
Sleaford Grn	28 B2
Smith St	16 C5
Solesbridge Clo	18 B1
Solesbridge La	18 B1
Somers Way	23 F3
Sonia Clo	21 H5
Sotheron Rd	16 C2
Souldern St	16 A5
South App	26 D2
South Cottage Gdns	18 B3
South Park Av	18 B3
South Rd	17 C3
South View Rd	27 H5
South Way	12 A3
Southfield Av	15 E2
Southsea Av	16 A4
Southwold Rd	14 D1
Sparrows Herne	23 E4
Sparrows Way	23 F4
Spencer Walk	18 D3
Spring Crofts	22 D1
Spring Gdns	13 F5
Springfield	23 G4
Springfield Clo	20 B3
Springfield Rd	13 E3
Springwell Av	18 C6
Springwell La	24 D2
Spur Clo	12 B3
Stag La	17 B4
Stamford Rd	16 B1
Stanbury Av	14 A1
Standfield	11 G5
Stanley Rd	16 D4
Stanmore Rd	14 C3
Staplefield Clo	28 C6
Station App, Carpenders Pk	28 B2
Station App, Chorleywood	17 C2
Station App, Hatch End	28 D6
Station App, Northwood	27 E6
Station App, Watford	14 A6
Station Rd, Rickmansworth	19 F5
Station Rd, Watford	16 B1
Steeplands	23 E3
Stevens Grn	23 F5
Stewart Clo	12 D1
Stockers Farm Rd	25 F2
Stockport Rd	17 C5
Stones Alley	16 B4
Strangeways	12 B6
Stratford Rd	16 A1
Stratford Way	14 B4
Stud Grn	13 E2
Summerfield Rd	12 D5
Summerhouse La	24 D6
Summerhouse Way	11 H5
Sunnyhill Rd	24 A5
Sussex Rd	14 A5
Sutcliffe Clo	23 F1
Sutton Rd	16 C3
Swallow Clo, Bushey	23 E4
Swallow Clo, Rickmansworth	19 E5
Swanston Path	28 A2
Swiss Av	14 A6
Swiss Clo	14 A6
Sycamore App	20 C3
Sycamore Clo, Bushey	15 G4
Sycamore Clo, Garston	13 E4
Sycamore Rd	20 C3
Sydney Rd	21 E3
Sylvia Av	28 C5
Talbot Av	22 B3
Talbot Rd	19 F6
Tamworth Clo	26 C5
Tanglewood Clo	23 H6
Tanners Hill	12 D1
Tanners Wood La	11 H5
Tavistock Rd	15 E3
Teal Dri	26 C6
Telford Clo	13 G4
Temple Clo	14 B4
Temple Gdns	26 B3
Terrace Gdns	16 B1
The Avenue, Bushey	22 C1
The Avenue, Hatch End	28 D5
The Avenue, Northwood	26 C5
The Avenue, Watford	16 A1
The Beeches	18 B3
The Birches	23 F2
The Boulevard	20 D3
The Briars	23 H4
The Broadway, Hatch End	28 D6
The Broadway, Watford	16 D3
The Brow	13 E2
The Bucklands	18 C5
The Byeway	25 H1
The Chase	21 E2
The Climb	18 D4
The Cloisters	19 F5
The Close, Bushey	22 D2
The Close, Moneyhill	18 D6
The Clump	18 C3
The Common	23 H6
The Comyns	23 F5
The Conifers	13 F4
The Coppice	21 H4
The Courtway	28 C1
The Crescent, Abbots Langley	11 H5
The Crescent, Croxley Green	20 A4
The Crescent, Watford	16 C5
The Dell	27 E1
The Drive, Rickmansworth	19 E4
The Drive, Watford	12 B6
The Fairway, Abbots Langley	12 B2
The Fairway, Eastbury	27 E3
The Four Tubs	23 G3
The Gardens	14 B4
The Garth	12 A3
The Glebe	13 G2
The Glen	26 D6
The Gossamers	13 H4
The Graylings	12 B2
The Green	19 H2
The Greenway	18 C5
The Harebreaks	14 C1
The Hideaway	12 D1
The Highlands	18 D5
The Hoe	28 B1
The Hornets	16 B5
The Lake	23 F4
The Larches	22 B2
The Leas	15 G3
The Malm	25 G1
The Maltings	12 A3
The Marlins	27 F4
The Mead	28 C2

The Mount	18 D4	Trundlers Way	23 G4	Warren Rd	23 F5	Winchester Way	20 A3
The Oaks	21 H6	Tucker St	16 C6	Warwick Clo	23 H4	Winchfield Way	19 E5
The Paddocks	18 B2	Tudor Av	15 E1	Warwick Way	20 C2	Windermere Clo	17 C3
The Pantiles	23 G4	Tudor Dri	15 F2	Water La	16 D5	Windmill Dri	19 H4
The Parade,		Tudor Manor Gdns	13 G2	Waterfield	17 C5	Windmill La	23 G5
Carpenders Park	22 B6	Tudor Walk	15 F1	Waterman Clo	21 G4	Windmill St	23 H4
The Parade, Watford	16 B3	Tudor Way	18 C6	Waters Dri	19 G6	Windsor Rd	14 D2
The Pastures	21 H5	Tunnel Wood Clo	14 B1	Watford Field Rd	16 D6	Windsor Way	18 C6
The Pathway	22 A4	Tunnel Wood Rd	14 B1	Watford Heath	22 A4	Winton App	20 C3
The Pelhams	13 G5	Turnbery Ct	28 A2	Watford Rd,		Winton Cres	20 B3
The Queens Dri	18 B5	Turner Rd	23 F1	Abbots Langley	12 A4	Winton Dri	20 B4
The Readings	18 B1	Turners Orchard	17 D3	Watford Rd,		Witney Clo	28 D5
The Retreat	11 E6	Tylersfield	12 D1	Croxley Green	20 A4	Woburn Clo	23 F2
The Ridgeway	14 A1			Watford Rd,		Wolsey Rd	26 D1
The Rookery	21 G5	University Clo	22 D1	Northwood	27 F6	Woodcock Hill	25 G3
The Roughs	27 F2	Uplands	19 G4	Wayside Av	23 G3	Woodfield Av	27 E3
The Roundway	21 E4	Upper Highway	12 A2	Weall Green	13 E2	Woodfield Rise	23 G3
The Rutts	23 G4	Upper Hill Rise	18 C4	Wedgewood Clo	26 D5	Woodford Rd	16 C1
The Spinney	14 C3	Upper Hillview Rd	28 D6	Wellesley Av	27 F4	Woodgate	13 E3
The Square	14 C1	Upper Hitch	28 C1	Wellington Rd	16 B1	Woodgate Cres	27 G5
The Squirrels	23 F2	Upper Paddock Rd	22 B3	Wellstones	16 B4	Woodhall Gate	28 B6
The Studios	22 D2	Upper Tail	28 C2	Wendover Way	23 F2	Woodhall La	28 B2
The Turnstones	13 H6	Upton Lodge Clo	23 F4	Wensum Way	19 E6	Woodhall Rd	28 B6
The Water Gate	28 B1	Upton Rd	16 B4	Wentworth Clo	14 B2	Woodhouse Eaves	27 G4
The Willows,		Uxbridge Rd		Wessex Dri	28 C6	Woodhurst Av	13 G4
Rickmansworth	24 D1	(Hatch End)	28 D3	West Dri	13 E5	Woodland Dri	14 B3
The Willows, Watford	21 G5	Uxbridge Rd,		West St	16 B1	Woodland La	17 D1
The Woods	27 G4	Money Hill	24 C2	West Way	18 D6	Woodland Rd	24 A4
Third Av	13 G5			Westbury Rd,		Woodlands Dri	11 E2
Thirlmere Gdns	26 C5	Vale Rd	22 B2	Northwood	27 E3	Woodlands Rd,	
Thorn Av	23 F5	Valency Clo	27 F3	Westbury Rd,		Bushey	22 B2
Thorndyke Ct	28 D6	Valley Rise	13 E3	Watford	16 B6	Woodlea Gro	26 D5
Thornhill Rd	26 C3	Valley Road	18 C3	Westfield Av	15 E1	Woodmans Yd	16 D5
Thorpe Cres	21 H5	Valley Walk	20 C3	Westfield Pk	28 D6	Woodmere Av	15 F2
Thrums	14 C1	Vega Cres	27 G4	Westland Rd	16 B2	Woodpecker Clo	23 F5
Thrush Grn	19 E5	Vega Rd	23 F4	Westlea Av	13 H6	Woodridge Way	27 E5
Tibbles Clo	13 H5	Vera Ct	22 A4	Westwick Ct	13 F4	Woodridings Clo	28 C6
Tibbs Hill Rd	11 H4	Verdure Clo	13 H2	Wharf La	19 G6	Woodshots Meadow	20 C3
Tichborne	24 A4	Vernon Rd	22 B1	Wheelwright Clo	23 E3	Woodside	12 D6
Timberidge	19 E2	Verulam Pass	16 B1	Whippendell Rd	16 A5	Woodside Rd,	
Titian Av	23 G4	Vicarage Rd	16 A6	Whisper Wood	18 D1	Northwood	27 G6
Tollgate Clo	18 B2	Victoria Clo	19 E5	White Gates Clo	19 H2	Woodside Rd,	
Tolpits Clo	21 E3	Victoria Rd,		White Hill	26 A5	Woodside	13 E1
Tolpits La	20 B6	Bushey	23 E4	Whitelands Av	17 B1	Woodstock Rd	23 H3
Toms La	11 E3	Victoria Rd,		Whitfield Way	18 B6	Woodville Ct	14 B4
Townfield	19 E5	Watford	14 D2	Whitwell Rd	13 G5	Woodwaye	21 H5
Townsend Way	27 F6	Villiers Rd	22 B3	Widgeon Way	13 H6	Woodwicks	24 A4
Treacy Clo	23 F5	Violet Way	19 E2	Wieland Rd	27 G6	Wren Cres	23 F4
Treetops Clo	26 D4	Vivian Clo	21 G6	Wiggenhall Rd	16 B5	Wyatt Clo	23 G4
Trefusis Walk	14 A3	Vivian Gdns	21 G6	Wilcot Av	22 B3	Wyatts Clo	18 B1
Trevallance Way	13 G3			Wild Wood	26 D5	Wyatts Rd	18 B2
Trevose Way	28 A2	Wadham Rd	12 C1	Wildoaks Clo	27 F5	Wychwood Way	27 F6
Trident Rd	12 D4	Wagon Way	19 E1	Wilford Clo	27 E6		
Trinity Clo	27 E5	Walnut Grn	15 G4	William St	15 F5		
Trinity Hall Clo	16 D2	Walpole Cl	28 D2	Willow Dene	23 H4	Yarmouth Rd	14 D2
Trout Rise	18 D1	Walton Rd	15 F6	Willow End	27 G5	York Rd	16 D6
Troutstream Way	18 C2	Walverns Clo	21 H4	Willow La	21 F3	York Way	13 G6
Trowley Rise	12 B1	Warneford Pl	22 B2	Wimborne Gro	14 A1	Yorke Rd	20 A4